JN034079

Common Errors in English Writing
New Edition

読み・書く 英語表現のポイント15章

Haruo Kizuka
Roger Northridge

TSURUMI SHOTEN

Common Errors in English Writing
New Edition

Photo credits:
© sudowoodo – stock.adobe.com
© wifineko/PIXTA（ピクスタ）
© marumaru/PIXTA（ピクスタ）
© sasuke/PIXTA（ピクスタ）
© HYONAM/PIXTA（ピクスタ）
© Fast&Slow/PIXTA（ピクスタ）
© tarou/PIXTA（ピクスタ）
© Fast&Slow/PIXTA（ピクスタ）
© ken3679/PIXTA（ピクスタ）
© wooooooojpn – stock.adobe.com
© cba/PIXTA（ピクスタ）
© 今井空 /PIXTA（ピクスタ）
© Josiah/PIXTA（ピクスタ）
© denkei/PIXTA（ピクスタ）
© 花火 /PIXTA（ピクスタ）
　　［掲載順］

自習用音声について

音声はアメリカ人男性とイギリス人女性によるものです。

本書の自習用音声は以下より無料でダウンロードできます。予習、復習にご利用ください。
（2021 年 4 月 1 日開始予定）

http://www.otowatsurumi.com/0052/

URL はブラウザのアドレスバーに直接入力して下さい。
パソコンでのご利用をお勧めします。圧縮ファイル (zip) ですのでスマートフォンでの場合は事前に解凍アプリをご用意下さい。

はしがき

　本書はマクミランランゲージハウス (MLH) 社から 1992 年に発売されて以来ロングセラーとして版を重ねた *Common Errors in English Writing* の大幅な改訂新版として刊行するものです。

　今回の改訂新版でも日本語を英語にする場合の文法上の約束事を無視する誤りから、意味上の誤り、コロケーション（連語）の間違いや日英発想の違いによる誤りに至るまで日本人英語学習者の犯しやすい誤りの具体例はこれまでの方針通り編集掲載しています。

　今回の大幅な改訂の内容は以下の通りです。

・ユニット数を 20 から 15 に圧縮しました。

・旧版の Opening Dialogue を日本の文化・社会をテーマとしたショート・エッセイに変更し、Reading and Writing の授業にも適応できる内容構成としました。なお、エッセイではそのユニットで学ぶ日本人英語学習者が誤りを犯しやすい語句について旧版と同様にボールド体で表記してあります。

・Exercise を全面的に新しい問題に差し替え、Exercise B については問題形式も改めました。

　各ユニットの冒頭エッセイの著者は、旧版の Opening Dialogue を書いてくれた研究社『新和英大辞典』の執筆者の一人であるイギリス人の Roger Northridge 氏です。今回は日本での長い生活と日本文化についての知識に裏打ちされた興味深いエッセイを書いてくれました。

　これからますます AI を活用した自動翻訳ソフトが進化していくことだと思いますが、自動翻訳ソフトに頼っていては英文を書く力も読む力も付きません。このテキストを用いた授業を受ける学生の皆さんが真の英語力を身につけるための地道な努力を続けてくれることを願っています。

2020 年 9 月

木塚　晴夫

CONTENTS

> ▶ **salary** と **wage** はどう違う？
> *There is a gap between the average salaries of women and men.*

🎧 Glass Ceiling
1

Traditionally, throughout Japan's feudal period, men ruled households with absolute authority. According to a Japanese proverb, fathers were to be feared as much as earthquakes, **thunder** and fire. Women were largely confined to the home, and when they started to work outside in the Meiji period, their **wages** were typically only one third those of men. Even today, while the situation for women is slowly improving, there is still a 25% gap between the average **salaries** of women and men. 5

In many companies, women had lower status. It used to be the **custom** in **offices** for female **staff members** to serve tea for the men. It is still often assumed that women will soon quit their jobs to get married. Meanwhile, Japanese work practices 10 are the **enemy** of equality. Men work longer hours and rarely take **days off**. They spend less time at home, and are not in the **habit** of doing much housework. This makes it harder for women to work, because the cost of childcare is high, and if they put their careers first, their families may have to pay the price.

Japanese women also have a low level of participation in politics, and make 15 up only about 4% of company executives. On TV news programs it is generally men who discuss difficult subjects like **economics**, while female announcers seem to have a more ornamental role. At work, women have to pay careful attention to their clothing and appearance. Recently, women working in department stores complained that they were not allowed to wear glasses. Apparently, **customers** 20 may think they look "unfeminine" and "too intelligent." Indeed *rikejo*, or "science girls," still face some prejudice. Despite their strength in science subjects, far fewer women than men are employed in the manufacturing and chemical industries.

Today, however, it is well understood that these attitudes can cause **damage** to women's prospects. Many companies are making efforts to improve conditions for working women, and the situation is gradually changing for the better.

25

★ Notes ★

1 **feudal period**「封建時代」／ 2– **as much as** 〜「〜と同程度の」／ 14 **pay the price**「犠牲を払う」

Watch the words

_1._ 「雷」は lightning か thunder か？

○ **Lightning** hit the mountain lodge, injuring two climbers.
× _Thunder_ hit the mountain lodge, injuring two climbers.

★ 日本語の「雷」は「雷鳴と稲妻」を含む言葉だが、英語では lightning「稲妻」と「thunder」を分けて使う。

_2._ salary と wage はどう違う？

○ The **salary** of a college professor is not high.
× The _wage_ of a college professor is not high.

★ salary は「主として知的な仕事に対して長期間にわたって定期的に支払われ固定給」。wage は「主として肉体的な労働に対して支払われる時間給・日給・週給などの賃金」なお、米用法では wage は wages と複数形で使われることが多い。

_3._ 「会社」はいつも company とは限らない。

○ I don't go to the **office** on Saturday.
× I don't go to the _company_ on Saturday.

★ company は an association of people carrying on business（事業を営む人々の集合体）なので、日本語の「会社へ行く」は go to the company とは言えない。go to the office か、もっと一般的な go to work とする。

_4._ economics と economy の違いは？

○ I major in **economics**.
× I major in _economy_.

★ 「学問としての経済」は economics。「国の市場に出回る資金、商業活動、産業の運営を表す経済」は economy。

_5._ 「習慣」は custom か habit か？

○ I regard smoking as a bad **habit**.
× I regard smoking as a bad _custom_.

★ いくら多くの人が行っていてもそれが「個人の習慣」の場合は habit。「国または社会の習慣」が custom。ただし、custom も次の例文のように「慣行、慣例」の意味では個人に用いられる。It is Professor Gold's custom to leave the door of his office open when coeds visit him.

6. 集合名詞を正しく使おう。

○ It was a mistake made by **one of my staff members**.
○ It was a mistake made by **a member of my staff**.
× It was a mistake made by *one of my staffs*.

★ staff は「職員全体」を指す集合名詞なので、one of my staffs. のような使い方はできない。audience, committee, crew, family などの集合名詞も使い方が難しいので注意が必要。

7. 「敵」は enemy 以外のこともある。

○ My **opponent** in the men's singles final is Goro.
× My *enemy* in the men's singles final is Goro.

★ 「戦争している敵」、「人類の敵」などという場合の「敵」は enemy だが、「競争相手」を意味するときの「敵」は opponent。

8. 「休み」はいつも vacation とは限らない。

○ I took a **day off** and moved house yesterday.
× I took a *one-day vacation* and moved house yesterday.

★ vacation は Christmas vacation, summer vacation のようにある「一定期間の休暇」を意味する言葉なので、two-week vacation とは言えても、one-day vacation とは言えない。holiday は主として法律や習慣で日常の仕事を休むように決められた日で、Martin Luther King Day is a holiday in the United States. のように用いられる。なお、英用法では holiday は summer holidays のように vacation と同じような使い方もする。

9. 「客」にもいろいろある。

○ The department stores were crowded with **customers**.
× The department stores were crowded with *guests*.

★ デパートや商店の「客」は customer。招待された人、ホテルや旅館の「客」は guest と使い分けられる。なお、弁護士、会計士などの「客」は client と言う。

10. 「損害・被害」はどんなに大きくても damages は誤り。

○ The coming typhoon will cause heavy **damage** to the rice crops for this year.
× The coming typhoon will cause heavy *damages* to the rice crops for this year.

★ 「損害」の意の damage は不可算名詞で、damages は「損害」ではなく「損害賠償金」。

Exercises

A-1. Choose the right words:

1. (Lightning, Thunder) rolled in the distance.

2. Tom is running a large trading (company, office).

3. My weekly (salary, wage) is 40,000 yen.

4. The government is taking steps to stimulate the (economy, economics).

5. The Japanese have been keeping this old (custom, habit) for many years.

6. My (family, families) are all tall.

7. He is the strongest (enemy, opponent) I have played against.

8. This inn has a lot of (customers, guests) this evening.

9. Let's take a (day off, vacation) tomorrow and go to Hakone.

10. (Damage, Damages) from that earthquake amounted to a billion yen.

A-2. Correct errors if any:

1. We are expecting five customers for dinner this evening.

2. Bathing in the river is a religious habit in this village.

3. There was a large clap of lightning soon after it began to rain.

4. I think they are salary earners.

5. I think I am my own worst enemy.

6. His speech appealed to wide audiences.

7. He has chosen to study economy instead of political science.

8. You should have a day off since you have been working so hard for the past two weeks.

9. The court awarded her one million yen in damage.

10. What time did you leave the company yesterday evening?

B. Fill in each blank with one word to complete the sentence:

1. 弟のアルバイトの仕事は、給料があまり高くありません。

   My brother's part-time job does not offer (　　　) (　　　　) (　　　　)
   (　　　　).

2. 彼女は故郷の証券会社に勤めています。

   She works (　　　　) a securities (　　　　　　) (　　　) (　　　　)
   (　　　　　).

3. 山本さんは働き者で滅多に休暇を取りません。

   Mr. Yamoto is a hard (　　　　) and rarely takes a (　　　) off.

4. 私は君の敵ではなく味方です。

   I am (　　　) (　　　) (　　　　) (　　　　) your friend.

5. 昨日の夕方雷が山小屋に落ち、登山者３人が怪我をしました。

   (　　　　　　) hit the mountain hut (　　　　) (　　　　),
   injuring three climbers.

6. あわてていたのでメガネを会社に忘れてきてしまいました。

   I was in such a hurry that I (　　　) (　　　) (　　　　) in the
   (　　　).

7. この国ではこの時期にプレゼントを交換するのが習慣です。

   It is the (　　　　) in this country to (　　　　) presents (　　)
   (　　) (　　　) of the year.

8. あの水害はこの地域の経済に重大な損害を与えた。

   The flood (　　　　　) caused serious (　　　　　) (　　) the
   (　　　) of this district.

9. このラーメン店は評判がよくて、いつも 20 人以上のお客さんが列に並んで店に入る順番を
   待っている。

   This ramen shop is (　　　) popular that (　　　　) (　　　) 20
   (　　　　) are always standing (　　) line, waiting their (　　　)
   to enter it.

10. このボートのクルーの一員になるのが私の長年の夢でした。

It was my long-cherished dream to be (　　　) (　　　) (　　　　　) of this boat.

C. Translate into English:

A: 高校の時化学部の一員だった円城寺さゆりさんを覚えている？

「化学部」chemistry club

B: うん。製薬会社の研究所に勤めているんだろう。

「製薬会社」pharmaceutical company

A: 彼女、4月1日に所長に昇進したそうよ。

「所長」director

B: それはビッグニュースだ。今日でも、女性に、十分能力を発揮できる機会を与える日本の会社は多くないからね。

A: とにかく、近いうちに彼女の昇進祝いをしましょうよ。

B: それはいい考えだ。恩師にも来られるか声をかけてみるよ。

「声をかける」get in touch with

A: ....

....

B: ....

....

A: ....

....

B: ....

....

A: ....

....

B: ....

....

Unit 2
冠詞の誤り

▶ 可算名詞でも冠詞がつかない慣用表現

Tastes and opinions will differ from person to person.

A Sense of Belonging

3

Japan is an island nation, isolated by **the Japan Sea** on one side and **the Pacific Ocean** on the other. This may be what has given it such a unique cultural identity. Living in village communities, on which they depended for survival, people also developed a strong sense of belonging to a group. Even today, most people derive their sense of identity from the group to which they belong. As suggested by   5
the expression *uchi no kaisha*, the company provides a sense of belonging, rather like a family.

But this means there is also a strong pressure to conform. People find it difficult to leave the office before their colleagues, even if there is no work to do. In American companies, workers expect to be paid **by the hour** for any overtime work they do,   10
while in Japan people do a great deal of unpaid overtime. Although progress is being made towards a better work-life balance, it is still common to eat **dinner** and drink with colleagues after work, and many workers don't take paid holidays.

In Western societies, it is considered natural that tastes and opinions will **differ from person to person**, and everyone is encouraged to express their   15
individuality. In Japan, however, there is **a proverb** that says "the nail that sticks out gets hammered down." If you behave too differently from others, you may receive **advice** to fall in line. Recently it was reported **on TV** that an 18-year old schoolgirl sued her school for harassment. The school claimed her dark brown hair was **the wrong color**, and repeatedly made her dye it black to look like everyone   20
else.

★**Notes**★

見出し **A Sense of Belonging**「帰属意識」／ 13 **take paid holidays**「有給休暇を取る」／ 16– **the nail ... down**「出る杭（釘）は打たれる」／ 19 **sued ~ for ...**「〜を…で訴えた」

Watch the words

1. There is the park. と言えるか？

　　○ There is **a park** near my house.
　　× There is *the park* near my house.

　　　★ there is (are) の後には初めて話題になる物がくるので、原則として the が付く名詞や固有名詞は使えない。

2. a good advice とは言えない。

　　○ He gave me good **advice**.
　　× He gave me *a good advice*.

　　　★ advice, information, news, progress などの名詞は不可算名詞なので、その直前に不定冠詞を付けることはできない。どうしても 1 つの advice と言いたい場合は a piece of advice。

3. 「自動車で」は by car か in a car。

　　○ We went home **by car**.
　　○ We went home **in a car**.
　　× We went home *by a car*.
　　× We went home *by the car*.

　　　★ 一般的に、「ある交通機関を利用して」という場合は〈by+ 無冠詞の交通機関名〉、例えば by car, by plane, by train とする。しかし、「ある交通機関に乗って」と「乗って」に重きが置かれるときは、in a car, in a plane, in [on] a train と言える。 冠詞・所有格が乗り物の前に付いているときは by a car のように by は使えない。

4. 川・海・運河には定冠詞が付く。

　　○ Let's build a "bridge" over **the Pacific Ocean**.
　　× Let's build a "bridge" over *Pacific Ocean*.

　　　★ 川・海・運河には定冠詞が付くが、湖は Lake Biwa のように無冠詞で使われる。

5. 計量・数量の単位を表すときは〈by+ 定冠詞 + 単位を表す名詞〉。

　　○ We have rented the boat **by the hour**.
　　× We have rented the boat *by hour*.
　　× We have rented the boat *by an hour*.

★ 計量・数量の単位を表すときは〈by+ 定冠詞 + 単位を表す名詞〉で、不定冠詞や無冠詞では使えない。

6. 〈right+ 名詞〉の前の冠詞は定冠詞。

○ I think you have made **the right decision**.
× I think you have made *a right decision*.

★ 〈right+ 名詞〉及び〈wrong+ 名詞〉の前には不定冠詞でなく定冠詞が用いられる。

7. 一般的な食事の前は無冠詞。

○ Have you eaten **breakfast** yet?
× Have you eaten *a breakfast* yet?

★ 一般的な食事の前には定冠詞も不定冠詞も付かない。ただし、修飾語が付くと、a light breakfast, a wonderful dinner, the lunch we had at that restaurant のように冠詞を付けて使う。

8. 「テレビ」は TV か the TV か？

○ What's on **TV** now?
× What's on *the TV* now?

★ TV は「テレビ放送」意味するときは無冠詞。「テレビ受像機」を意味するときは冠詞が必要。ただし、ラジオで聴くは listen to the radio または listen to (something) on the radio で冠詞が必要。

9. 「人間」は man。

○ **Man** cannot live by bread alone.
× *A man* cannot live by bread alone.

★ 「人間、人類」を意味するとき man は無冠詞。ただし、man は元来「男性」を表す言葉なので、男女を含めた人類全体を指すのは差別的であるとされ、近年は human beings や humans を使うことが多い。

10. 「花から花へ」は from flower to flower。

○ Butterflies were flying **from flower to flower**.
× Butterflies were flying *from a flower to a flower*.
× Butterflies were flying *from the flower to the flower*.

★ face to face, from morning to [till] night, from door to door, from flower to flower, from land to land, arm in arm, side by side などは使われている名詞が可算名詞でも、慣用表現なので冠詞は付けない。

Exercises

A-1. Choose the right words:

1. "Is this Mr. Johnson's residence?" "Sorry, but you've got (a, the) wrong number."

2. Is there (a, the) big bank in your neighborhood?

3. Did you go to Hakone (by train, by the train)?

4. You should realize that customs differ from (a land to a land, land to land).

5. Keiko's English has recently made (a rapid, rapid) progress.

6. Turn on (radio, the radio), will you?

7. What time do you usually have (a lunch, lunch)?

8. What's (a, the) matter? You aren't ill, are you?

9. Jean lives near (Lake, the Lake) Michigan.

10. I think this is the worst disease known to (a man, man).

A-2. Correct errors if any:

1. Janet has told me an interesting piece of news.

2. He was driving over 100 kilometers an hour.

3. Taro caught me by arm and didn't let me go.

4. My grandfather was killed in World War II.

5. Suddenly he came up with a right answer to the question.

6. Will you turn down TV?

7. A dinner we had at the Chinese restaurant yesterday was delicious.

8. I saw Goro and Kumiko walking arm in arm this afternoon.

9. He goes to the work by bicycle.

10. Suddenly I came the face to face with Professor Smith.

B. Fill in each blank with one word to complete the sentence:

1. 毎日散歩するのは体によい。

   (　　　　　　) (　　　　) (　　　　　　　) every day is good (　　　　　) (　　　　　　)
   (　　　　　　).

2. お母さんは夕食に鶏肉を料理しています。

   Mother is cooking (　　　　　　) (　　　　) (　　　　　).

3. 家の近くに公園があり、春になるとそこでいろいろな花が咲きます。

   There is (　　　) (　　　　　　) near my house and various (　　　　　　　)
   of (　　　　　) come out in spring.

4. この頃は多くの人がガンで死亡します。

   Many (　　　　　　) die (　　　　) (　　　　　　　) these days.

5. 私はその事件に関する情報をたくさん持っています。

   I (　　　　) a lot of (　　　　　　　) (　　　　　) that incident.

6. 子供の頃はよく利根川で泳いだものです。

   I (　　　　　) (　　　　) swim (　　　) (　　　　　) Tone River when I was (　　　)
   (　　　　　).

7. 彼は一人っ子で大学卒業後は家業を継ぐ予定です。

   He is an (　　　　　) (　　　　　　) and is to (　　　　　) (　　　　　) the family
   (　　　　　　) after he (　　　　　　) (　　　　　) college.

8. 昨夜遅くまで起きていたので朝から頭が痛い。

   I (　　　) (　　　　) (　　　　　　) last night, so I have (　　　　) (　　　　)
   (　　　　　　) since this morning.

9. 人前で話すときは聴衆の目を見なさい。

   When you speak (　　　) (　　　　　　), you should look your (　　　　　　)
   (　　　) the eye.

10. 昨夜久しぶりにタイガースとジャイアンツの試合をテレビで見ました。

    I (　　　　　　) the game (　　　　　　) the Tigers and the Giants (　　　　)
    (　　　) last night for the first time in many weeks.

C. Translate into English:

A: あなたは、ここ数週間日夜一生懸命働いてきたので、今週末にあなたと奥さんに夕食をご馳走するわ。

B: 本当ですか。それを聞いて家内は大喜びすると思います。

A: 土曜日の夕方は都合はいいですか。

B: はい。土曜日は何の予定もありません。

A: 大学時代の友人の１人がグルメで、おいしいレストランに関する情報をたくさん持ってるから聞いておくわ。

「グルメ」gourmet

B: 評判のレストランでのおいしい夕食のことを考えただけでよだれがでそうです。

「よだれがでる」make one's mouth water

A: ....

....

B: ....

....

A: ....

....

B: ....

....

A: ....

....

B: ....

....

Unit 3
動詞の誤り (1)

▶ **put on** と **wear** の違い

After the bath, you can put on a yukata

 Onsen

Japan is a mountainous nation, with active volcanoes and many fast-flowing rivers. It is frequently **struck** by typhoons, bringing torrential rain. But the geothermal activity and the abundance of water means that *onsen*, or hot springs, are to be found in almost all rural areas. For visitors to Japan, **enjoying** a *rotenburo*, or open-air bath, while looking out over the natural scenery, is an experience not to be missed. 5

There is a great variety of hot spring baths. Some are so small that only two or three people can enter at a time, while others are as large as a swimming pool. Of course one doesn't visit a hot spring to **go swimming**. They are strictly for relaxation, and you can soak in the healing waters for hours on end, enjoying a sense of peace and calm. It is easy to drop in at an onsen without a reservation. If you 10 forget to **bring** a towel, most hot springs will **lend** you one. After the bath, you can **put on** a *yukata*, or light summer kimono, and continue to relax for hours.

Modern *onsens* offer visitors many types of entertainment. At a new natural hot spring in Tokyo, there is even a "viewing spa" where you can **watch** sports on a big-screen TV while soaking in the bath. Public baths in Japan have always been a 15 place where everyone felt equal, and divisions were relaxed. It is not unusual, while sitting naked in the bath, to find oneself **discussing** serious issues with complete strangers.

Since the 1970s, most homes have had their own baths, and the *sento*, or public bath, has declined in popularity. But even the bath in a Japanese home is like a 20 miniature *onsen*. Soaking in the bath after a hard day's work is an essential part of the daily routine. Once they **come to know** the Japanese bathing culture, foreigners never want to abandon it, while Japanese residents in foreign countries, who **have**

grown up with the Japanese bath, feel deprived of this wonderful custom, which **has become** so much a part of the Japanese identity.

25

★ Notes ★

9 **on end**「続けて」／ 16 **divisions**（分割されている）湯船のこと。

Watch the words

1. play はすべての運動競技に使えるわけではない。

　○ John often plays basketball and **goes swimming**.
　× John often plays basketball and *swimming*.

　　★ 元来 play は野球、テニス、バスケットボールなどの球技をするときの「する」に相当する
　　　動詞で、運動でも swimming や wrestling とは結びつかない。

2. enjoy は通例他動詞として用いられる。

　○ Did you **enjoy the party** last night?
　○ Did you **enjoy yourself at the party** last night?
　× Did you *enjoy at the party* last night?

　　★ 日本語では、普通、「パーティーは楽しかったですか」と尋ね、「パーティーを楽しみました
　　　か」とはあまり言わないので、Did you enjoy at the party? のように言う人がかなりい
　　　るが、このような文では enjoy は他動詞なので目的語が必要で、すぐ後に前置詞が来るこ
　　　とはない。enjoy が自動詞として使われるのは、口語で、飲み物などを「さあどうぞ」とす
　　　すめたり、旅行に出かける人に「楽しんでいらっしゃいね」などというときだけ。

3. 「…する（ように）なる」に become は用いない。

　○ That's how I **came** to know her.
　○ That's how I **got** to know her.
　× That's how I *became* to know her.

　　★ become は We became good friends. や Our friendship has become stronger. の
　　　ように次に名詞や形容詞を伴い「…になる」の意で用られるが、「…する（ように）なる」は
　　　come to ... または get to ...。

4. 「野球を見る」は see [watch] baseball。

　○ I often **see** baseball on TV.
　○ I often **watch** baseball on TV.
　× I often *look at* baseball on TV.

　　★ 「…を見る」に相当する英語には look at、see、watch があるが、look at は主に静止し
　　　ているものを見るときに用いる。運動などを見るときは see または watch。

5. 「襲う」は attack とは限らない。

○ Kyushu is often **hit** by typhoons.
○ Kyushu is often **struck** by typhoons.
× Kyushu is often *attacked* by typhoons.

★ 「襲う」というとすぐ attack を頭に浮かべる人が多いが、attack は「(敵、痴漢、病気などが) 襲う、激しく攻撃する」場合に用いられる動詞で、「(嵐、台風、地震などが) 襲う」ときは hit や strike を使う。

6. 「大人になる」は grow up。

○ When I **grow up**, I would like to be a teacher.
× When I *grow*, I would like to be a teacher.

★ grow は「人が大きくなる、(背などが) 伸びる」で、「成長して大人になる」は grow up。

7. まぎらわしい bring と take の使い方。

○ When you come to my house, why don't you **bring** your kids?
× When you come to my house, why don't you *take* your kids?

★ bring は「持ってくる、連れてくる」take は「持って行く、連れて行く」が原義だが、相手の方に「持って行く、連れて行く」ときは take でなく bring を用いる。

8. put on と wear の違い。

○ She was **wearing** a white sweater when I first met her.
× She was *putting on* a white sweater when I first met her.

★ 「着る」に相当する英語には put on と wear があるが、前者は動作を、後者は状態を表す。

9. 「…について議論する」は discuss about ... か？

○ We **discussed** environmental destruction till late at night.
○ We **talked about** environmental destruction till late at night.
× We *discussed about* environmental destruction till late at night.
× We *talked* environmental destruction till late at night.

★ 日本語の「…について」に引かれて、discuss about ... としがちだが、discuss は他動詞なのですぐ後ろに目的語をとり、about という前置詞を入れると誤りになる。一方、talk は自動詞なので前置詞なしで目的語と結びつくことはない。

10. lend と rent と borrow を区別して使おう。

○ I missed today's lecture. Could you **lend** me your notes?
○ I missed today's lecture. May I **borrow** your notes?
× I missed today's lecture. Could you *borrow* me your notes?
× I missed today's lecture. Could you *rent* me your notes?

★ lend は「無料で貸す」、rent は「有料で貸す、有料で借りる」、borrow は「借りる」。それ故 borrow を使って「貸してくれますか」というときは、主語が I になる。

Exercises

A-1. Choose the right words:

1. He was (attacked, hit) by a car yesterday.

2. "(Put on, Wear) these new shoes. Hurry up!"

3. My sister often (looks at, watches) TV till late at night.

4. I (grew, grew up) three centimeters last year.

5. May I (borrow, lend) ¥10,000 yen?

6. Kent likes to (play wrestling, wrestle).

7. She (came to, became) a Diet member at the age of 30.

8. "So you live here in Tokyo? What (brought, took) you to Japan?"

9. When you were young, didn't you go out and (enjoy, enjoy yourself)?

10. Don't (talk, talk about) serious issues with strangers.

A-2. Correct errors if any:

1. We'll go swimming as soon as you finish your household chores.

2. Where were you born and brought up?

3. We have nothing to talk this evening.

4. It's getting late. I'll bring you home.

5. Let's go and look at the football game.

6. I discussed the problem with my classmates.

7. I usually wear a black suit when I go to work.

8. Here's your hamburger. Enjoy!

9. Many college students lend rooms near the campus.

10. When it becomes to cooking, Keiko knows what's what.

B. Fill in each blank with one word to complete the sentence:

1. 今日の午後ボーリングしないか。

   How about (　　　　) (　　　　　　　) this afternoon?

2. 私たちは何時間も地球温暖化について議論した。

   We (　　　　　) (　　　　　) warming (　　　　) hours.

3. 弟も私もネクタイにはうるさく、よく見てから買います。

   My brother and I are particular about ties and (　　　　) (　　) them very

   carefully (　　　　　) we buy (　　　　　).

4. 昨夜はずいぶん雨が降ったが、今日は快晴なので車を借りてドライブに行こうよ

   We (　　　) a lot of rain last night, but since we (　　　　　) fine weather

   today, let's (　　　) a car and go (　　　) a drive.

5. この部屋は暗いけどすぐに慣れますよ。

   This room is dark, but you'll soon (　　　　　　) accustomed (　　　) it.

6. ジャックはニューヨークで生まれ、東京で育ったので英語も日本語も話せます。

   Since Jack (　　　　) (　　　　　) in New York and (　　　　) (　　　) in

   Tokyo, he speaks (　　　) English (　　　　) Japanese.

7. 空が曇ってきた。傘を持っていった方がいいよ。

   The sky is (　　　　　) cloudy. You'd better (　　　　　) an umbrella with you.

8. その恐ろしいウイルスは神経組織を襲うと言われています。

   The dreadful virus is (　　　　) to (　　　　　) the (　　　　　) system.

9. 彼女は急いで化粧して部屋から出て行った。

   She (　　　) on her makeup in a hurry and (　　　　　) (　　　　) of the room.

10. 今年の夏は故郷の長野に帰って楽しみたい。

    I'd (　　　) (　　　) go home to Nagano and (　　　　　) (　　　　　)

    this summer.

🎧 **C.** Translate into English:

6

A: 誕生パーティに招いてくれてありがとう。とても楽しかったわ。夕食はとてもおいしかったわ。

B: 気に入ってよかった。妻は料理が得意なんだ。

A: あなたは幸運なだんなさんだね。どうやって彼女と知り合ったの？

B: うん、4年前に交換留学生として初めて日本に来たとき彼女の家にホームステイしたんだ。

A: そう。彼女は英語は話せたの？どうやってコミュニケーションとったの？

B: ちょっとだけね。だから最初は主に身振り手振りでさ。でも着実に彼女の英語が上達して今では政治問題についてだって英語で議論できるんだ。

A: ....

....

B: ....

....

A: ....

....

B: ....

....

A: ....

....

B: ....

....

Unit 4
動詞の誤り (2)

▶ よく間違える **rise** と **raise**

Families raise colorful carp streamers from their homes.

🎧 Events and Festivals
7

In my small village in Shinshu, each year is punctuated by annual events, which mark the seasons as well as bringing the community together. A meeting **is held** in March, at which the head of the village for the following year **is elected**. At the annual festival in April, the village shrine is decorated, the priest dresses up in splendid robes, makes offerings to the gods, and recites a very long chant which ₅ he **has memorized** by heart. For the Children's Festival in May, families **raise** colorful carp streamers from their homes. At the Obon festival in August, flowers are placed at family graves, and elderly villagers invite family members from the city to **come** and visit them.

Festivals are usually centered on temples and shrines. Some have spectacular ₁₀ processions of floats, pulled by local people dressed in traditional costumes, and tourists to Japan find them a delight. At any time of the year, you can usually find a festival to visit if you **look it up** in a festival calendar. Japan is said to have some 200,000 festivals, and their continuity is quite remarkable. Some, like Kyoto's Aoi Festival, **have been held** for a thousand years, and neither the costumes nor the ₁₅ rituals have changed. Even if the procession **gets caught in** a rainstorm, festivals are seldom called off, while at Suwa's Onbashira Festival, participants **are** often seriously **injured** as they slide down a hill on massive logs, yet the festival still goes on.

Can Japan retain its festival culture? Rural communities no longer have enough ₂₀ young people to carry the heavy *mikoshi*. Meanwhile, major festivals like Kyoto's Gion Festival and Tokushima's Awa Odori have run into financial difficulties. Many temples and shrines are also in trouble, and people are losing interest in them.

19

Young people in the cities may have **graduated from** university but not be able to **tell** you how a shrine differs from a temple. But let us hope they will continue to celebrate Hinamatsuri, Tango no Sekku, and Shichi-Go-San. If Japan were to lose its traditional culture of festivals and *nenchu gyoji*, it would be a great loss to the nation and to the world. 25

★ Notes ★

1 **Shinshu**「信州」信濃地方。／ 7 **carp streamers**「鯉のぼり」／ 17 **Suwa's Onbashira Festival**「諏訪の『御柱祭』」長野県の諏訪大社で 7 年ごとに行われる勇壮な祭り。

Watch the words

1. 「行く」は go とは限らない。

　　"Can you come to our house this evening?"
　○ "Sure. I'll **come** about 8 o'clock."
　× "Sure. I'll *go* about 8 o'clock."

　　★ 上記の文は「今夜僕の家に来られるかい？」と問われたのに対し、「8 時頃行くよ」と答えているのだが、話相手の所へ「行く」は go でなく come。

2. 日本語の他動詞が英語では自動詞のことがある。

　○ I **graduated from** the University of California in 2015.
　× I *graduated* the University of California in 2015.

　　★「大学を卒業する」という場合、日本語の「卒業する」は他動詞だが、このとき使われる英語の graduate は、標準文法では自動詞なので、from を入れないと誤りになる。ただし、目的語がない I graduated in June, 2015. は正しい英文。このような間違いを起こしやすい英単語には add, depend, major, operate, succeed, wait などがある。

3. よく間違える raise と rise。

　○ If you have a question, **raise** your hand.
　× If you have a question, *rise* your hand.

　　★ raise は他動詞で rise は自動詞。同じように、lay と lie、set と sit もよく混用されるので注意が必要。

4. choose と elect と select の違いは？

　○ There are three clubs I'm interested in, but I can **choose** only one.
　○ There are three clubs I'm interested in, but I can **select** only one.
　× There are three clubs I'm interested in, but I can *elect* only one.

★ choose と select は共に「(いくつもの中から) ～を選ぶ」を意味するが、select の方が choose よりもフォーマルな単語で、よく考えて慎重に選ぶときに使われる。elect は「投票して選ぶ」の意で、We elected Jack (as) captain of our team. のように用いる。

5. The meeting opens. は「会議が開かれる」ではない。

○ The meeting **is held** from January 10 to 15.
× The meeting *opens* from January 10 to 15.

★ 会議や展示会などが「開かれる、開催される」は be held で open は使えない。open は「会議」などと一緒に使われる場合は The meeting opened last Monday. の ように「始まる」を意味する。

6. 道を「教える」に teach は使えない。

○ Please **tell** me the way to Tokyo Station.
○ Please **show** me the way to Tokyo Station.
× Please *teach me* the way to Tokyo Station.

★ 「教える」でも teach は「知識・技能を習得させる」の意なので、「道」などを教える場合には使えない。道を「口頭で教える」ときは tell、「地図を描いたり自分で案内して教える」場合は show。

7. memorize と remember は意味が違う。

○ I **memorized** five new English words yesterday.
○ I **learned** five new English words **by heart** yesterday.
× I *remembered* five new English words yesterday.

★ 同じ「覚える」でも「暗記する、記憶する」に相当する英語は memorize か learn by heart。remember は「記憶している、忘れずにいる」の意で、Do you remember the day we first met? のように使う。

8. check, look up, examine, investigate の区別。

○ Please **look up** in this schedule when the next train leaves.
○ Please **check** in this schedule when the next train leaves.
× Please *examine* in this schedule when the next train leaves.
× Please *investigate* in this schedule when the next train leaves.

★ 同じ「調べる」でも、(辞書・電話帳・時刻表などにあたって)「調べる」は look up、(状態・性質がどうなっているかを知るために「調べる」は examine、(事実関係や原因などについて警察などが組織的に) 調べる」は investigate。check は、組織的に調べる場合以外ほとんどどんなときにも「調べる」の意で使える。

9. 雨に「遭う」に meet は使えるか？

○ I **was caught in** the rain on my way home yesterday.
○ I **got caught in** the rain on my way home yesterday.
× I *met* the rain on my way home yesterday.

★ meet は主として、「(2 人またはそれ以上の人が偶然または約束して) 会う」ときに用い

られ、「（雨などに）遭う」に be [get] caught in を使う。事故に「遭う」は have [meet with] an accident.

10. be wounded=be injured ではない。

○ He **was** seriously **injured** in the car accident.
○ He **was** seriously **hurt** in the car accident.
× He **was** seriously *wounded* in the car accident.

★ be wounded は「（武器・凶器などにより）怪我をする、負傷する」の意なので、（事故で）怪我をする」ときには使えない。「（事故で）怪我をする、負傷する」場合は be injured か be hurt。

Exercises

A-1. Choose the right words:

1. The government is said to be planning to (raise, rise) taxes.

2. Why don't you (lay, lie) down on my bed for a while if you don't feel well?

3. The chairwoman (held, opened) the meeting by welcoming everybody.

4. His report will be (checked, looked up) next week.

5. The coach (elected, selected) five candidates for the national team.

6. Please (teach, tell) me how to play the violin.

7. The doctor (examined, investigated) my stomach.

8. We are late because we (met, were caught in) a traffic jam.

9. The actor had to (memorize, remember) his lines by the end of this week.

10. Was your father (injured, wounded) when the building collapsed?

A-2. Correct errors if any:

1. As far as I memorize, I met him in San Francisco in 2019.

2. Commodity prices have recently been raising.

3. The teacher could not answer my question.

4. The ball is going to you. Please pick it up and throw it to me.

5. Teach me when the next bus is scheduled to come.

6. He has recently opened an office in Los Angeles.

7. Are you majoring economics?

8. Who laid the foundation of modern Japan?

9. Despite her painstaking efforts, she couldn't succeed losing weight.

10. His jokes made us laugh.

B. Fill in each blank with one word to complete the sentence:

1. 昨夜は本州中大雪でした。雪は東京でも 15 センチ近く積もりました。

   We (　　　　) (　　　　　　) (　　　　　　　) throughout Honshu last night. The snow (　　　　　) nearly 15 centimeters deep even in Tokyo.

2. 私たちはもう 30 分以上彼女を待っていますが、電車が遅れているのかしら。

   We've already (　　　　　) (　　　　　　) (　　　　) her for more than half an hour. I wonder if her train is late.

3. 最近マナーを守らない若者が増えているのは嘆かわしい。

   It's regrettable that the number of young people who do not observe manners (　　　　) recently (　　　　) (　　　　　).

4. 警察はどうやってその男が私のアパートに侵入したかを注意深く調べています。

   The police are (　　　　　　　　) carefully (　　　　) the man entered my apartment.

5. ピートはチャランポランに見えるけど、当てにして大丈夫だ。彼は決して友人を裏切らないから。

   Pete looks irresponsible, but you can (　　　　　　) (　　　) (　　　　). He never fails a friend.

6. 今度の株主総会では誰が次期社長に選ばれると思う？

   Who do you think (　　　) (　　　) (　　　　　　) next president at the coming general meeting of stockholders?

7. 私は 2018 年にあなたと軽井沢で過ごした楽しい日々をまだ覚えています。

I (　　　) (　　　　　　　) the happy (　　　) I spent (　　　) (　　　)
in Karuizawa in 2018.

8. 昨日学校からの帰り道、にわか雨に遭いびっしょりになりました。

I was (　　　　) (　　　) a shower and got drenched to the skin (　　　)
my (　　　) home from school yesterday.

9. 話したいことがあるんだけどいつ会いに行ったらいい？

I have something to (　　　) (　　　　) you about. When can I (　　　　)
to (　　　) you?

10. もしイギリスの大学で勉強できるなら、政治を専攻したい。

I'd (　　　) (　　　) (　　　　) (　　　　) political science if I can study at
a British university.

A: ジーンさんが昨夜事故に遭って入院したそうよ。

「入院した」be hospitalized

B: 本当か。どんな事故だったんだ？

A: 彼女が歩いていたとき飛ばしてきた自転車にぶつけられ、大怪我をしたのよ。

B: 3 月に大学を卒業し、京都で開かれる 1 週間の国際会議に出席したらカリフォルニアへ帰国すると言っていたのに。

A: 病院に見舞いに行きたいので、彼女が入院している病院を調べておくわ。

B: そうしてくれ。そしてその病院への行き方を教えてくれ。

A: ....
....

B: ....
....

A: ....

....

B: ....

....

A: ....

....

B: ....

....

Unit 5
時制の誤り

▶ 日・英時制のずれ

We will do our best to find it.

🎧 Lost and Found
9

If you lose something in Japan, you are more likely to get it back than in any other country on earth. One day last year, I dropped my wallet in the car park before getting into my car. Realizing it was missing, I called the local police station. "Oh," said the police officer, "Someone **turned up just now** with a wallet. Why don't you come and pick it up?" The wallet was full of money, but nothing was missing, ₅ and I gave the man a reward. When I **lost** my camera in London **some years ago**, I had a different experience. When I called the police, they said, "Well, **we will do** our best to find it, but you have very little hope of ever seeing it again."

In Japan, most people **have known** since they were in elementary school that, if they **find** something on the street, they should immediately take it to the ₁₀ nearest koban. All kinds of items are handed in, and stored for 3 months if no one **comes** to collect them. It does not matter how old they are or how bad they look. If an item of clothing **smells** bad, it **will be washed** before being stored. Every day, thousands of people come to lost and found centers in Tokyo to pick up their belongings. They are asked some simple questions such as where and when they last ₁₅ saw the item, and what it looks like, before they can claim it back. As many as three quarters of all lost items find their way back to their owners.

The custom of handing in lost property **has existed** since long before anyone **was born**. Indeed, Japan **has had** some form of "lost and found system" for hundreds of years. Foreigners often wonder why the Japanese are so honest. Perhaps ₂₀ people like to do good deeds for others because they feel others may do the same for them. It is also said that people believe "the sun is always watching you." They are certainly very conscious of the "eyes of others." In Europe and America, on the other hand, we have the saying, "Finders keepers, losers weepers."

26

4 **turned up**「現われた、姿を見せた」／ 24 **"Finders keepers, losers weepers"**「見つけた者が持ち主、失くした者は泣き寝入り」

Watch the words

1. 知覚動詞は通例進行形を作れない。

○ This steak **tastes** good.
× This steak *is tasting* good.

★ hear, see, smell, taste, notice などの知覚動詞は、Mother is smelling the roses in the garden. のように、～しているという有意志の動作を示すとき以外は進行形は作れない。

2. 過去を表す副詞（句）には原則として過去形を。

○ She **bought** a bicycle the day before yesterday.
× She *has bought* a bicycle the day before yesterday.

★ yesterday, the day before yesterday, last week, 10 years ago など過去を表す副詞（句）があるときは動詞は過去形。

3. just now には原則として過去形の動詞を。

○ He **returned** to the office just now.
× He *has returned* to the office just now.

★ just now は通例 a short time ago を意味するので、普通過去の動詞を用いる。ただし、I'm tied up just now.（今忙しい）のように、just now が at this moment を意味するときは現在形が使われる。

4. 現在の習慣・反復的動作に進行形は使わない。

○ I **get up** at seven every morning.
× I *am getting up* at seven every morning.

★ 現在の習慣・反復的動作は現在時制で表し、原則として現在進行形は使わない。

5. 時や条件を表す副詞節の中の未来は現在時制で。

○ I'll stay home if it **rains** tomorrow.
× I'll stay home if it *will rain* tomorrow.

★ 時や条件を表す副詞節の中で、未来を述べる場合は現在時制を用いる。

6. have は無意志的動作や状態を示すときは進行形を作れない。

○ I **have had** a headache since this morning.
× I *have been having* a headache since this morning.

★ be 動詞や have は、普通は状態や無意志的動作を示すので進行形を作れない。ただし、We are having a garden party next Saturday. のように have が動作を表すときは進行形も可能である。

7. 疑問詞の when で始まる文に通例現在完了形は使えない。

○ When **did** you **see** Mary?
× When *have* you *seen* Mary?

★ 過去の時を尋ねる疑問詞の when で始まる文には通例現在完了形は使えない。

8. 日・英時制のずれ (1)

○ My father died before I **was born**.
× My father died before I *am born*.

★ 日本語では「父は私が<u>生まれる</u>前に亡くなりました」と現在時制のような使い方をするが、英語では before I was born と過去形にしないと誤りである。

9. 日・英時制のずれ (2)

○ I **will do** my best in the coming contest.
× I *do* my best in the coming contest.

★ 日本語では「ベストを尽くすだろう」とは言わず、「ベストを尽くす」と言うので、現在時制にしがちだが、未来のことなので、ここでは I will do my best ... としなければいけない。

10. 日・英時制のずれ (3)

○ I **have known** Judy since she was a small child.
× I *know* Judy since she was a small child.

★ 日本語では「私はジュディを小さな子供の頃から知っています」と現在時制で表すので、I know ... と言いがちだが、英語では現在完了形にしないといけない。

Exercises

A-1. Choose the right words:

1. I will wait here till you (come, will come) back.

2. When I was a small boy, I (swam, was swimming) in this river almost every day.

3. I will come to your party if you (invite, will invite) my girlfriend too.

4. I think you (succeed, will succeed) if you try again.

5. Mary (is resembling, resembles) her mother.

6. The suspect (is looking, looks) like a famous actor.

7. How long (do you study, have you studied) English?

8. At that time those islands (belonged, were belonging) to Spain.

9. I (am, will be) 20 on my next birthday.

10. This milk (is tasting, tastes) sour.

A-2. Correct errors if any:

1. When have you been to China?

2. I see if I can find time to help you this evening.

3. Are you still loving your girlfriend?

4. What are you thinking about the economic situation today?

5. Here came the bus. Let's get on.

6. I think I have met her before.

7. Goro has come back from Australia just now.

8. We are always going to Hakone on weekends.

9. Do you know when Jack will come home this evening?.

10. Did you ever see pandas?

B. Fill in each blank with one word to complete the sentence:

1. 両親が帰ってきたらすぐ出かけます。

    I'll go out (   ) soon (   ) my parents (   ) home.

2. 昨夜遅くから高熱が続いているんです。

    I (   ) (   ) a high (   ) since last night.

3. 富士山がいつ噴火するかを予測するのは難しい。

    It is difficult to predict (   ) Mt. Fuji (   ) (   ).

4. その事故については何も知りません。たった今帰宅したばかりですから。

    I don't know anything about the accident. I (   ) (   ) just now.

5. 雨が止んだらハイキングに行こう。

    Let's go hiking if it (   ) (   ).

6. ホイッスルが鳴ったぞ。もうすぐ次のレースが始まるよ。

    There goes the whistle. The next race (   ) (   ) soon.

7. アメリカへは去年行きましたが、まだカナダへ行ったことはありません。

    I went to the United States last year, but I (   ) (   ) (   ) to Canada.

8. 遅れてごめん。家を出ようとしているときに電話があったもので。

    I'm sorry I am late. I (   ) just about to leave home when I (   ) a call.

9. 「自分の部屋のお掃除をわすれないでね」「うん」

    "Don't forget to clean your room." "(   ), I (   )."

10. 母は作ったばかりのケーキの味見をしています。ちょっと甘すぎると言っています。

    Mother (   ) (   ) the cake she (   ) just made. She says it's a bit too sweet.

C. Translate into English:

A: 日本にどのくらい住んでいるのですか。

B: 3年です。2018年に来ました。

A: どうして日本に来たのですか。

B: 子供の頃日本のアニメ映画を2、3見て、そのとりこになったのです。大人になったら日本
でアニメ映画の勉強をしたいと思いました。

    「〜のとりこになる」be captivated by ~

A: そうですか。私も日本のアニメ映画に目がないんです。その中には私が生まれる前に作られ
たのに未だに人気のあるものがいくつかありますよ。

    「〜に目がない」have a weakness for ~ ; be crazy about ~

B: 知ってますよ。子供の頃からそれらは何度も繰り返し見ていますから。

A: ....

  ....

B: ....

  ....

A: ....

  ....

B: ....

  ....

A: ....

  ....

B: ....

  ....

Unit 6
〈動詞＋名詞〉の誤り

▶ 「注目を集める」に collect や gather は使えるか？

***The candidacy speech attracted
the attention of the world.***

🎧 *Omotenashi*
11

Shortly after an earthquake and tsunami **caused devastating damage** to the Fukushima nuclear power plant, Japan put in a bid to host the Olympic Games. The candidacy speech by Christel Takigawa **attracted the attention** of the world when she mentioned *omotenashi* as one of Japan's national assets. In the following years, many tourists **have taken the advice** of travel agents to experience 5 Japan's legendary hospitality, and Japan has **made rapid progress** towards its target of admitting 40 million tourists a year. Recently, more people have even come from overseas to **have medical checkups** in Japan, because of the personalized care and treatment they receive.

Tourists are impressed by the way shops, restaurants and hotels in Japan **give** 10 **such consideration** to customers' needs. It seems the customer is treated like a god. If you arrive at a department store at opening time, the employees line up and bow to you as you enter. When you sit down in a restaurant, you are immediately given a glass of water and a hot towel. It makes a pleasant contrast with some countries, where shop assistants will not serve you because they are talking on the 15 phone, or waiters can't be bothered to **pass you the menu**, and then give you a dirty look when you don't leave them a tip.

Service in Japan goes the extra mile. Restaurants produce cakes for people celebrating their birthdays, and hotels provide Kit Kat "*kitto katsu*" chocolates to university entrance candidates to make sure they don't **fail their exams**. If you 20 are lost on the street, people may take the trouble to **draw you a map**, or even walk with you to your destination. Many citizens in Japan **join SGG clubs** of volunteers, who guide tourists around the country for free.

32

Where does this spirit of *omotenashi* come from? Some say it originates in the tea ceremony, and the philosophy of Sen no Rikyu, who taught that you should anticipate the needs of your guest and give them a memorable experience without expecting anything back. It seems that "service" is not just a transaction, where you get what you pay for, but something that transcends economic concerns.

★ **Notes** ★

3 **candidacy speech**「立候補スピーチ」／ 18 **goes the extra mile**「なお特別な努力をする」／ 22 **SGG club**＝Systematized Goodwill Guide Club「善意通訳者の会」

Watch the words

1.「する」は do とは限らない。

○ She has **made** rapid **progress** in her English.
× She has *done* rapid *progress* in her English.

   ★ 日本語は多くの場合、「散歩する」、「進歩する」のように、名詞に「する」を付けて簡単に動詞が作れるが、英語では名詞に do を付けて動詞化するケースは少なく、do 以外の動詞が結びつくことが多い。

2.「損害を与える」は give damage と言えるか？

○ The coming typhoon will **cause [do]** heavy **damage** to the rice crops for this year.
○ The coming typhoon will **inflict** heavy **damage** on the rice crops for this year.
× The coming typhoon will *give* heavy damage to the rice crops for this year.

   ★「忠告を与える」、「チャンスを与える」はそれぞれ give advice、give a chance と言えるが、「損害を与える」は cause (do, inflict) damage で、give damage は誤り。

3.「幸せな生活を送る」は have [lead, live] a happy life。

○ After he retired, Ken **had [led, lived] a happy life** in Canada.
× After he retired, Ken *sent a happy life* in Canada.

   ★「生活を送る」の「送る」に send は使えない。なお、have [lead,live] と life が結びつくときは、通例 life の前に不定冠詞と形容詞を付ける。

4.「忠告を聞き入れる」を receive advice とするのは誤り。

○ He **accepted** my advice and went on to graduate school.
○ He **followed** my advice and went on to graduate school.
○ He **took** my advice and went on to graduate school.
× He *received* my advice and went on to graduate school.

★ 忠告を受け入れたり、忠告にしたがったりするとき advice と結びつく動詞は、accept, follow, take で、receive advice とは言えない。「要求を受け入れる」場合も demand と結びつく動詞は accept。「試験を受ける」も receive an exam でなくて、take an exam。

5. 「試験に落ちる」は drop in an exam と言えるか？

○ She **failed (in)** the English exam.
○ She **flunked** the English exam.
× She *dropped in* the English exam.

★ 「試験に落ちる」は fail (in) an exam か flunk an exam で drop in an exam は誤り。drop は I will drop English next year.（来年は英語は棄てます［履修しません］）、The manager has dropped me from the new team.、I dropped 1 kilogram last month. のようにな使い方なら正しい。

6. 「かく」でも「書く」と「描く」では違った動詞を使う。

○ **Draw a circle** here.
× *Write a circle* here.

★ 文字や文章を「書く」場合は write で、絵・丸・地図などを「描く」は draw。

7. 「注目を集める」に collect や gather は使えるか？

○ The news **attracted my attention**.
○ The news **drew my attention**.
× The news *collected my attention*.
× The news *gathered my attention*.

★ 「人の注目を集める」は attract [draw] someone's attention で、動詞に collect や gather は使えない。

8. 「取る」に get, take 以外の動詞が使われるときがある。

○ Please **pass** me **the salt**.
× Please *get* me *the salt*.
× Please *take* me *the salt*.

★ 「免許を取る」は get a license、「休暇を取る」は take a vacation のように「取る」にはよく get や take が使われ、食卓で「塩を取ってください」と言うときは、Please pass me the salt. と動詞には pass が用いられる。

9. 「入る」は enter とは限らない。

○ I **joined the** tennis **club** last week.
× I *entered the* tennis *club* last week.

★ 「部屋に入る」は enter the room だが、「クラブに入る」は join the club。「風呂に入る」は take a bath。

10. 「受ける」に have, do, suffer が使われることがある。

    ○ I **had a** medical **checkup** yesterday.

    × I *took a* medical *checkup* yesterday.

    ★ 「教育を受ける」は receive education、「試験を受ける」は take an exam だが、「健康診断を受ける」は have a (medical) checkup、「追試を受ける」は do a makeup、「被害を受ける」は suffer damage と言う。

Exercises

A-1. Choose the right words:

1. I (followed, received) your advice and went to see a doctor yesterday.

2. You called me when I was (entering, taking) a bath.

3. After his retirement my uncle (sent, led) a frugal life in the country.

4. How come you (did, made) such an easy mistake?

5. Did the earthquake (do, give) some damage to your company?

6. The teacher (called, got) my attention to the problem.

7. The agreement (made, put) an end to the civil war.

8. You should think carefully before you (do, make) such an important decision on your future.

9. Can you (pass, take) me the bag by your feet?

10. Who advised you to (enter, join) our team?

A-2. Correct errors if any:

1. Are you determined to win the current difficulties?

2. Do you know who runs this restaurant?

3. Study hard and give a good example for your brothers.

4. We are placing great hopes on developing a market in Africa.

5. Who's going to break the news to your parents?

6. You should do every possible effort to pass the finals.

7. My brother did the trouble to pick me up at the airport.

8. Can you write me a map of the way to his house?

9. Don't jump to the conclusion that the accident was caused by the negligence of the night watchman.

10. If the minister fails to fill his campaign promises, he will lose in the next election.

B. Fill in each blank with one word to complete the sentence:

1. その国では需要に合うだけの石油がなかった。

   There was not enough oil to (   ) (   ) (   ) in that country.

2. 彼は独創性に富んでいるのできっと起業家として成功するよ。

   I'm sure he (   ) (   ) success as an entrepreneur since he is
   (   ) (   ) original ideas.

3. 山本氏はその醜聞の責任を取って取締役会長を辞任した。

   (   ) responsibility (   ) the scandal, Mr. Yamamoto resigned as chairman of the board.

4. その委員会は日本の学校はもっと口語英語の勉強に力を入れるべきだとの結論に達した。

   The committee has (   ) at the conclusion that Japanese schools
   should (   ) more emphasis (   ) the study of oral English.

5. あの指導者はいつも他国に迷惑をかけている。

   That leader is always (   ) trouble (   ) other countries.

6. 前もって電話をしてくれればあなたの依頼に応じられると思います。

   I think I can comply (   ) (   ) (   ) if you call me in advance.

7. その洪水は何百人もの命を奪った。

   The flood (   ) (   ) of lives.

8. 彼は日本で高校を終えてからアメリカ留学の試験をうけた。

   After (   ) high school in Japan, he (   ) an examination
   (   ) studying in the United States.

9. 新しい抗がん剤の開発は世界中の多くの人の関心を集めている。

The (   ) of the new anti-cancer drug is (   ) the
attention of many people around the world.

10. 彼女は先週英語の試験に落ちたので来週追試を受けるつもりだ。

As she (   ) in the English exam last week, she (   ) (   )
do a make-up next week.

C. Translate into English:

12

A: 3月に引っ越そうと思っている。私たちの町が去年の秋大きな台風に見舞われ、私のアパートも大損害を受けたの。

B: それは気の毒だったね。どこに移るか決めたのかい？

A: いや、未だなの。大学の近くのアパートに移りたいんだけどいいアパートを見つけるのに苦労しているわ。

B: ブラウン教授に助言を求めたらどう？　友人の1人が、彼の助言に従って「国際会館」に住んでいるよ。

「国際会館」International House

A: そうしてみるわ。もしそこに住めたら大学へは歩いて10分で行ける。その上いろいろの国から来た学生と意見交換ができるわ。

B: おそらく、主に英語でコミュニケーションをとることになるから君の英語は急速に上達するよ。

A: ....

....

B: ....

....

A: ....

....

B: ....

....

A: ....

....

B: ....

....

Unit 7

準動詞（不定詞・動名詞・分詞）の誤り

▶ **look forward to** のあとは通例準動詞

Tourists from overseas always look forward to traveling on the shinkansen.

🎧 Being on Time
13

One appealing aspect of Japanese society is that it operates with clockwork precision. When I lived in Tokyo, I can **remember setting** my watch by the arrival times of trains. Recently, a scandal erupted when a train left the platform a mere 25 seconds ahead of schedule. Tourists from overseas always **look forward to traveling** on the shinkansen, which has a yearly average delay time of only 5 30 seconds. A mere 3 minutes after trains arrive at their destination, the cleaning teams are already **busy making** them spick and span. Exactly 7 minutes later, they **have finished cleaning** the entire train, ready for new passengers to board. Other facilities also seem to keep a close eye on the clock. When you **go shopping** at a department store, the doors open at 10 AM on the dot. 10

In Japan, people expect you to be on time for meetings, and you **had better arrive** 5 minutes early. Everyone **avoids being** late, even though people don't seem to **mind staying** in meetings for hours on end. When the members of my village assemble for grass-cutting in the summer, work is supposed to begin at 5:30 AM. However, **arriving at the work site** before 5:30, **I found** that everyone 15 had already started. Working in a company, you can't **afford to** arrive late, or leave early. One company employee recently had his pay docked for leaving his desk 3 minutes before lunchtime. Even Cabinet ministers have to be punctual. Some time ago, when a minister arrived 10 minutes late for a committee meeting, the opposition parties protested for 5 hours and **had him publicly apologize**. 20

Is punctuality intrinsic to Japanese culture? As late as the Meiji Period, it is said that people were far less strict about time. Indeed, when foreigners **hear Japanese spoken**, they sometimes have difficulty telling whether the tense is present or future. Perhaps punctuality reflects a desire to carry out tasks with faultless precision. And it must also come from a feeling of not wanting to let the side down, or create a bad impression. Most people, it seems, would much rather wait for others than make others wait for them.

★ Notes ★

1– **with clockwork precision**「時計じかけのような正確さで」／ 7 **spick and span**「清潔な、こざっぱりした」／ 17 **had his pay docked**「賃金を削られた」／ 21 **intrinsic**「固有の」／ 21 **As late as the Meiji Period**「つい明治の頃は」／ 23– **difficulty telling whether the tense is present or future**「時制が現在形なのか未来形なのか見分ける難しさ」／ 25 **let the side down**「（友や家族などを）がっかりさせるようなことをする、恥をかかせる」

Watch the words

1. finish は不定詞を目的語にすることはできない。

○ Have you **finished writing** a letter to your friend?
× Have you *finished to write* a letter to your friend?

> ★ 英語の動詞の中には不定詞を目的語にできないものがある。avoid, consider, delay, enjoy, escape, finish, mind, miss, postpone, practice, quit, resistなどその種の動詞である。

2. 一般の前置詞 to と不定詞を導く to を区別しよう。

○ I **am looking forward to hearing** from you soon.
× I *am looking forward to hear* from you soon.

> ★ 前置詞の to は、名詞や動名詞の前に置き、方向、限界、目的、結果、結合、比較などを示す場合と、〈to+ 動詞の原形〉で不定詞を示す記号のようになっている場合があるため、この両者をはっきり区別する必要がある。

3. 「… （するので忙しい）」は busy+doing。

○ She is **busy doing** the dishes now.
× She is *busy to do* the dishes now.

> ★ busyは、かつては busy+in+doing の型で使われていたが、現在では in を省いて用いるのが一般的。同じように、have difficulty [trouble]、have a good time、take turns などの後も、現在では in を省いて直接動名詞を続けることが多い。

4. 目的語が動名詞と不定詞では意味が違う動詞がある。

○ I **remember seeing** him before.
× I *remember to see* him before.

★ remember, forget, regret などは、目的語が動名詞のときはすでにしたこと、不定詞のときはこれからすることを表す。

5. 単に「泳ぎに行く」を go to swim とは言わない。

○ Did you **go swimming** yesterday?
× Did you *go to swim* yesterday?

★ go boating [fishing, camping, hunting, shopping, skating, skiing, swimming] などは一種の慣用句で、〈go+ これらの動詞の不定詞〉は普通使われない。ただし I often go to the nearby river to swim. のように go と不定詞の間に他の語句が入れば正用法である。

6. 使役動詞の 〈have+ 目的語〉の後は原型不定詞。

○ I'll **have him call** you back as soon as he comes home.
× I'll *have him to call* you back as soon as he comes home.

★ 使役動詞に have を使うときは〈have+ 目的語〉の後は原型不定詞。ただし、使役動詞に get が用いられると I'll get him to call you back as soon as he comes home. のように〈get ＋目的語＋不定詞〉となる。

7. had better の後は原型不定詞。

○ You **had better see** a doctor right away.
× You *had better to see* a doctor right away.

★ had better, would rather, cannot but, may well, may [might] as well の後は原型不定詞。

8. afford の目的語は不定詞。

○ I cannot **afford to buy** such an expensive house.
× I cannot *afford buying* such an expensive house.

★ 英語の動詞の中には動名詞を目的語にできないものがある。afford, agree, care, decide, expect, hesitate, learn, plan, promise, refuse, seek, wish などがその例である。

9. 「(目的語) が…されているのを知覚する」は〈知覚動詞 + 目的語 + 過去分詞〉。

○ **Have** you ever **heard** the Spanish language **spoken**?
× *Have* you ever *heard* the Spanish language *speak*?
× *Have* you ever *heard* the Spanish language *speaking*?

★ 「(目的語) が…されているのを知覚する」という文では、〈知覚動詞＋目的語＋過去分詞〉が正用法。

10. 独立分詞構文以外では、分詞の意味上の主語と主文の主語は一致する。

○ **Entering** the room, **I found** some footmarks on the floor.
× *Entering* the room, some *footmarks were found* on the floor.

★ 独立分詞構文以外では、分詞の意味上の主語と主文の主語は一致させなければならない。

Exercises

A-1. Choose the right words:

1. Have you decided (accepting, to accept) his offer?

2. I'll get my brother (pick, to pick) you up in front of Iidabashi Station.

3. I suggest that you postpone (to look, looking) for a job for a while.

4. Do you enjoy (to listen, listening) to classical music?

5. You'd better not (to eat, eat) that fish. It doesn't smell good.

6. We aren't used to (work, working) for six hours without a break.

7. When do you think you can finish (fixing, to fix) my car?

8. That old museum is worth (visiting, to visit).

9. He denied (to see, seeing) the scene of the crime.

10. Have you ever heard this children's song (sing, sung)?

A-2. Correct errors if any:

1. You shouldn't have let her to go.

2. She is accustomed to travel alone.

3. Did she promise to come to your birthday party?

4. Shall we postpone to leave early tomorrow morning if it rains?

5. I had a good time to play soccer last Saturday.

6. Do you regret not going on to graduate school?

7. I will never forget to visit you in San Francisco when I was a student.

8. Do you think this movie is worth to see?

9. What do you say to go on a hike tomorrow?

10. Can you make yourself understood in English?

B. Fill in each blank with one word to complete the sentence:

1. あなたがお皿洗いを終えたらすぐデパートへ買い物に行くわよ。

   We'll (   ) (   ) at a department store as soon as you
   (   ) (   ) the dishes.

2. 昨夜飲み過ぎて今日は働く気がしない。

   I drank too much last night and don't feel (   ) (   ) today.

3. その問題を解くのに私たちはとても苦労した。

   We had a lot of difficulty in (   ) (   ) (   ).

4. 大学生の息子は暮れに私たちに会いに来ると約束していたが、アルバイトが忙しすぎて帰郷
   出来なかった。

   Our son, who is a college student, promised to (   ) (   ) (   )
   us at the end of the year, but he was too (   ) (   ) part-time
   to come home.

5. 朝食をすますと、私は始発電車に間に合うように急いで家を飛び出した。

   (   ) finished breakfast, (   ) rushed (   ) of the house to be in
   time for the first train.

6. 問題があったら遠慮なく僕の研究室に来なさい。

   Don't (   ) (   ) (   ) to my office if you have any
   problems.

7. 暗闇の中で私は突然自分の名前が呼ばれるのを聞いた。

   I suddenly heard (   ) (   ) (   ) in the dark.

8. その伝統ある都市は爆撃されるのを何とか免れた。

   The traditional city barely avoided (   ) (   ).

9. 今日の我々の相手は強敵なので、つまらないミスは許されない。

   Our opponent today is strong, so we (   ) afford (   ) (   )
   any careless errors.

10. 母はとても手先が器用なので、私は月に一度母に髪を切ってもらいます。

    My mother is very skillful with her hands, so I (   ) (   ) (   )
    (   ) by her once a month.

🎧 *C.* Translate into English:

14

A: わが社に入りたいんだって？それなら、まず第一にすべきことは禁煙だわ。

B: そういえば君の会社は厳格な禁煙方針を取っているんだね。テレビで見たのを覚えているよ。他にしてくれる忠告はあるかい？

A: そうね、あなたはいつも机に向かっていてあまり丈夫そうに見えないから毎日運動をして体調を整えておくことね。

「体調を整えておく」 get in shape

B: 忠告に従って、毎朝ジョッギングをすることにするよ。

A: あなたからよい知らせをもらうのを期待して待っているわ。

B: 入社試験の結果が分かったらすぐ電話するよ。

「結果が分かる」 learn the result

A: ....

....

B: ....

....

A: ....

....

B: ....

....

A: ....

....

B: ....

....

Unit 8
形容詞の誤り

▶ 狭いはいつも**narrow**とは限らない

Japan is a relatively small nation with little ethnic or cultural diversity.

 **Culture of Shame**

The anthropologist Ruth Benedict wrote an **interesting book** in which she defined Japanese culture as a culture of shame. From fear of shame, the Japanese behave according to how they think others will see them. They tend not to assert themselves, and **are often ashamed** to say what they really think, for fear of being laughed at. Perhaps it was because the Japanese had not developed an individualistic ⁵ culture of debate and democratic institutions that General MacArthur thought them **childlike**. And yet this "shame culture" proved to be extremely **effective** in creating a society where everyone acted in the common interest, making Japan a leading **industrial** power in the postwar years.

People seem **glad** to work in the service of society, and take very seriously ¹⁰ their duties to their family, neighbors and the group to which they belong. Actions by individuals reflect on the group, so if one member of a group does something socially unacceptable, the whole group is **embarrassed**. Since group harmony is more important than individual aspirations, people tend to be very **sensitive** to the views and feelings of others. Those who express opinions too different from the ¹⁵ group may be opposed or even ostracized. It is better to fit in than to be right, and the **sensible** choice is to keep your private self hidden. The separation of *tatemae* from *honne* is therefore very **convenient** if one wants to get on in society. It may be that this culture of shame has contributed to Japan's **economic** success, since people have a strong need to fulfil their obligations, and the expectations of others. This ²⁰ makes them perfectionists at work, and very **industrious**, since perfectionism is an **effective** insurance against criticism.

Japan's shame culture may have persisted because Japan is a relatively **small**

45

nation with little ethnic or cultural diversity, so standards of behavior are very clear. But is this now beginning to change? For some young people, these standards are 25 seen as too oppressive, and they avoid traditional employment, working in part-time jobs even if the pay is **low**. Perhaps future generations will seek to assert their individuality more, and this could greatly affect the nation's politics as well as its economy.

★ Notes ★

1 **Ruth Benedict**「ルース・ベネディクト」アメリカの文化人類学者 (1887–1948)。著書に *The Chrysanthemum and the Sword*『菊と刀──日本文化の型』(1946) など。／ 6 **General MacArthur**「マッカッサー元帥」第 2 次世界大戦後に日本を占領統治したアメリカの司令官。「日本人はまだ 12 歳の少年である」と言った。／ 16 **may be opposed or even ostracized**「妨害されるとか追放さえされたかもしれない」／ 16 **fit in**「(人) とうまくやっていく」／ 18 **get on in society**「社会で成功する、うまくいく」／ 22 **insurance against criticism**「非難防止の手段」

Watch the words

1. 「狭い」はいつも narrow とは限らない。

○ Japan is a **small** country.
× Japan is a *narrow* country.

★ narrow は主として「(幅が) 狭い」ときに使い、「(面積が) 狭い」ときは small を用いる。「広い」も「(幅が) 広い」ときは wide を、「(面積が) 広い」ときは big や large を使う。

2. 「安い」は cheap だが…

○ This price is **low**.
× This price is *cheap*.

★ 「(物が) 安い」は cheap だが、「(値段が) 安い」は low。「(物が) 高い」は expensive、「(値段が高い)」は high。

3. effective と efficient の違いは？

○ This medicine is said to be **effective** against lung cancer.
× This medicine is said to be *efficient* against lung cancer.

★ effective は「効果が期待できる、(薬などが) 効く」、efficient は「能率的な、効率が良い、有能な」の意。

4. 「経済的な」は economic か economical か？

○ This is a very **economical** car.
× This is a very *economic* car.

★ economic activity（経済活動）、economic situation（経済情勢）など、「経済（上）の」の意味の形容詞。一方、「経済的な、徳用の」は economical。

5. childish と childlike は意味が違う。

○ Nobody respects him because he is 30 but acts in a **childish** manner.
× Nobody respects him because he is 30 but acts in a *childlike* manner.

★ childish は大人に用いられると「大人げない、子供っぽい」と悪い意味を表す。一方 childlike「子供のような、純真な」の意の形容詞でよい意味で使う。

6. 「工業国」は industrial nation。

○ The leaders of the seven **industrial** nations met in Tokyo.
× The leaders of the seven *industrious* nations met in Tokyo.

★ industrial は「産業の、産業の発達した、工業の」、industrious は「勤勉な」の意。

7. 「感じやすい」は sensitive。

○ She is so **sensitive** that she is easily hurt.
× She is so *sensible* that she is easily hurt.

★ sensible は「知覚できる、分別がある、思慮がある」、sensitive は「過敏な、影響を受けやすい」の意の形容詞。

8. 「恥ずかしい」はいつも be ashamed とは限らない。

○ I **was embarrassed** when she asked me how old I was.
× I *was ashamed* when she asked me how old I was.

★ be ashamed は「（恥・罪・不面目を感じて）恥ずかしい」。それに対して be embarrassed は「（心が混乱して、どきどきして）恥ずかしい」。

9. 形容詞には人間しか主語にできないものがある。

○ **I was glad** to hear that you had passed the entrance exam.
× *It was glad for me* to hear that you had passed the entrance exam.

★ able, afraid, anxious, careful, eager, glad, interested, pleased, satisfied などは、人間以外を主語にすることはできない。

10. convenient は人間を主語にできない形容詞。

○ **Is** next **Sunday convenient** for you?
× *Are you convenient* next Sunday?

★ 人間を主語にできない形容詞には convenient のほかに、inconvenient, impossible, possible, satisfactory などがある。

Exercises

A-1. Choose the right words:

1. Everyone in his family is very (industrial, industrious).

2. I was (ashamed, embarrassed) when I saw food stains on my white shirt.

3. For a 30-year-old man his behavior was (childish, childlike).

4. Oranges are (cheap, low) at this time of the year.

5. It was (satisfactory, satisfying) to see my daughter win the close game.

6. (Is it possible for you, Are you possible) to finish your homework by six o'clock?

7. His efforts to improve the educational organization were very (effective, efficient).

8. (I will be able, It will be able for me) to solve the problem in an hour.

9. Several developing countries are now faced with an (economic, economical) crisis.

10. He is very (sensible, sensitive) to soybeans.

A-2. Correct errors if any:

1. Japan's industrial production declined last month.

2. Her hands are dainty and childish.

3. The TV program featured China's economical future.

4. He is very effective and always finishes his work before five.

5. It's difficult to move the piano through this narrow hallway.

6. The tuition at our university is very low.

7. Dogs are more sensible to odors than humans.

8. I was ashamed when I tripped and fell down the stairs.

9. It's pleased to see you for the first time in a couple of months.

10. We are necessary to fill out the application forms.

B. Fill in each blank with one word to complete the sentence:

1. 今年の夏、あなたが私に会いにロンドンに来てくださると聞いてとてもうれしいです。

   I'm ( ) ( ) ( ) ( ) that you are coming to see me in London this summer.

2. この道路はせまくて、くねくねと曲がっているんだから、慎重に運転してくれよ。

   This is a ( ) ( ) road, so be sure to drive carefully.

3. 来週夕食にお招きしたいのですが、何曜日がご都合がよいでしょう？

   We'd like to invite you to dinner next week. ( ) ( ) would be ( ) ( ) you?

4. こんな些細なことに腹を立てるなんて大人げないよ。

   It's ( ) ( ) ( ) to get angry over such a trivial matter.

5. 在宅勤務が増えているから私たちはもっと有効な時間管理法を見つけなければならない。

   Since working from home is increasing, we must find a ( ) ( ) ( ) of managing our time.

6. 多くの人が使えば使うほどスマートフォンは安くなるでしょう。

   The prices of smart phones will get ( ) ( ) ( ) as more and more people use them.

7. 彼女は夫にありとあらゆる悪態をついたことを恥じた。（〜に悪態をつく「call~names」）

   She ( ) ( ) ( ) calling her husband all the names she could think of.

8. この頃は着る物はほとんどインターネットで買います。そのほうが買い物に行くよりずっと便利だし経済的だから。

   I buy most of my clothes on the Internet these days. It's far ( ) ( ) ( ) ( ) than going shopping.

9. アメリカや日本やドイツのような工業国が直ちに効果的な政策を取らないと、世界の経済情勢はますます悪くなるでしょう。

   If ( ) nations such as the United States, Japan and Germany fail to take ( ) steps immediately, the world's ( ) situation will get worse and worse.

10. 野党のその議員は、首相は事実をありのままに言っていないと非難した。

The Diet member from the opposition party criticized the prime minister for
(　　　　) (　　　　　　　　　　) with the truth.

🎧 *C.* Translate into English:

B: 今朝はなぜマスクしているの？

A: 昨夜風邪を引いちゃった。クラスの誰にも移したくないのよ。教室はとても狭いでしょ。

　　「…を～に移す」pass ... on to ~

B: そうか。それは賢明だよ。それに、そのマスクをしていると君はかわいらしくて無邪気に見えるよ。

A: 自分のマスクを持っていないので、妹のを借りてきたのよ。何人かの男の子が私をからかって恥ずかしかったわ。

　　「～をからかう」make fun of ~

B: 鞄の中にビタミンの錠剤が入っているから何錠かあげるよ。僕も風邪には弱いんでいつも持ち歩いているんだ。風邪には効くし無害だからね。

A: ありがとう。高い値段で買ったんじゃないでしょね。

B: ....

....

A: ....

....

B: ....

....

A: ....

....

B: ....

....

A: ....

....

Unit 9
副詞の誤り

▶ 形容詞の最上級を修飾する副詞は？

Japanese food is now considered to be much the best for one's health.

 *Washoku*

A few decades **ago**, Japanese cuisine was not widely known outside Japan. In the UK, for example, there were a few Japanese restaurants in London, but their customers were mainly Japanese. Nowadays, however, noodle and sushi bars are springing up all over the country. Japanese foods like *tofu*, *miso*, *kombu* and bonito have **already** become so familiar that people keep them in their fridges. They 5 have come to enjoy Japanese food **very much**, for the subtlety of its tastes, the variety of the ingredients, and its emphasis on vegetables and fish rather than meat. While Indian, Italian and Chinese restaurants are also popular, Japanese food is now considered to be **much the best** for one's health.

The fact that Japan has a **very high** average life expectancy must have something 10 to do with the simple cooking styles, fresh ingredients, and well-balanced nutrition of Japanese cuisine. It makes use of fermented foods, which are good for the digestion, seaweed, which is packed with minerals, and many types of seafood. It also uses as many as 1500 different ingredients. Japanese food is widely considered to be healthy, but it is also valued for aesthetic and cultural reasons. Menus are chosen 15 according to the seasons, with a variety of wild plants still used in some dishes, and chefs work very hard on the presentation of meals.

Throughout the developed world today, people eat **too much** fast food, don't get enough vitamins and minerals, and don't take enough exercise **either**. Remarkably, however, Japan's food culture has been **almost** unaffected by these trends. It is 20 true that consumption of both rice and vegetables is declining, and "metabolic syndrome" has become an issue. Yet when people grab a bite to eat at a convenience store, it is likely to be an *onigiri*, which is considerably healthier than a hamburger, and when they get a drink from a vending machine, it is likely to be some variety of tea, which contains antioxidants, rather than a soft drink, laced with sugar. People seem to be resisting the rise of junk food, and continuing to value *washoku*, which has **recently** been designated by UNESCO as an Intangible Cultural Heritage. 25

★Notes★

3– **are springing up**「次々に生まれている」／ 4 **bonito**「カツオ」／ 12 **fermented foods**「発酵食品」／ 25 **antioxidant**「酸化防止剤」／ 25 **laced with sugar**「砂糖を加えられた」／ 27 **Intangible Cultural Heritage**「無形文化遺産」

Watch the words

1. very と much の違い。

　　○ It was **very** dark when I got home.
　　× It was *much* dark when I got home.

　　　★「大変」の意味で very または much を使うとき、形容詞の原級を修飾する場合は very、過去分詞を修飾するときは much。ただし、excited や interested のように心理状態とか感情を表す語のときは、それが形容詞と見なされ very が使われることがある。much で修飾可能な形容詞の原級は different のように比較級に準ずるものや afraid や alike のように叙述用法しかないもの。

2. hard の副詞は hardly ではない。

　　○ You should not work so **hard**.
　　× You should not work so *hardly*.

　　　★ hard それ自体で形容詞としても副詞としても使われる。hardly は「ほとんど…しない」の意の副詞。just と justly, late と lately, most と mostly のように、副詞の中には 2 つの形を持ち、それぞれ異なった意味で使われるものがある。

3. 形容詞の最上級を修飾する副詞は？

　　○ She is **much the best** student in our class.
　　○ She is **the very best** student in our class.
　　○ She is **by far the best** student in our class.
　　× She is *the much best* student in our class.
　　× She is *very the best* student in our class.

　　　★ 一般的には、形容詞の最上級を修飾する副詞は much だが、上例のように very が使われることがある。このときは much の場合と違い、定冠詞が very の前。

4. 肯定文では通例副詞の much は単独では用いない。

○ We enjoyed the party **very much**.
× We enjoyed the party *much*.

★ 肯定文では通例副詞の much は単独では用いない。very much のように他の副詞とともに使う。肯定文で単独で使えるのは much the same などの慣用句だけ。

5. 「まだ」の意の yet は主として否定文で使う。

○ I **still** hate our new French teacher.
× I hate our new French teacher *yet*.

★ 「まだ…である」と動作・状態の継続を表すときは still を使う。yet が肯定文で用いられるのは、The figures may yet be revised upward. のように、「やがて、いつか」の意で未来に言及するときである。yet は、否定文で「まだ（…でない）」という動作の未完了を表すときに使われる。

6. 驚きを表す「もう」は already。

○ It's still 5 o'clock. Have you eaten dinner **already**?
× It's still 5 o'clock. Have you eaten dinner *yet*?

★ Have you eaten dinner yet? は「夕食はもう食べましたか」という疑問文としては正しいが、「夕食はもう［こんなに早く］食べちゃったの」という驚きの気持が入っている場合の「もう」は yet でなくて already。

7. 否定文の「もまた」に too は使えない。

○ "I don't like onions." "I don't like them **either**."
○ "I don't like onions." "**Neither** do I."
× "I don't like onions." "I don't like them *too*."

★ too も either も「…もまた」を意味するが、too は肯定文で、副詞の either は否定文で使われる。上のような文では否定語の neither を使って Neither do I.（略式では Me neither.）もよく用いられる。

8. 現在を基点とした「前」は ago。

○ She visited Kyoto ten years **ago**.
× She visited Kyoto ten years *before*.

★ 現在を基点として「今から…前」は ago で、ago は常に期間を示す語句とともに用いられる。当然時制は過去である。一方 before は、期間を示す語句を伴うときは、「（過去の）ある時点から…前」で、Janet told me that she had met Ted a few weeks before. のように動詞の過去完了形とともに使われる。before が単独で用いられるときの動詞は現在完了・過去・過去完了のいずれもありうる。

9. recently は通例現在完了または過去時制と一緒に。

○ The number of foreign visitors to Japan **has recently been increasing**.
× The number of foreign visitors to Japan *is recently increasing*.

★ recently, lately, of late は一般に現在完了また過去時制の部で用いられる。現在時制のときは、recently の代わりに、nowadays や these days が使われる。

10. 副詞にもある定位置。

○ I was **almost** involved in the car accident.
× *Almost* I was involved in the car accident.

★ 文中における副詞の位置は、ほかの品詞に比べて比較的自由であるが、やはり定位置がある。形容詞・副詞を修飾する場合は被修飾語の前、頻度を示す副詞は動詞の前（be 動詞の場合は後、助動詞がある時は助動詞と動詞の間）などである。

Exercises

A-1. Choose the right words:

1. That animal lived two million years (ago, before).

2. "Have you finished writing your report?" "No, not (already, yet)

3. My Canadian friend went home last year, and I miss him (much, a lot).

4. I have eaten two hamburgers, but I am (still, yet) hungry.

5. The train was (much, very) delayed by the rainstorm.

6. I was (almost, mostly) hit by a car yesterday.

7. We arrived at the hotel very (late, lately) at night.

8. Global warming has become a (very, much) serious problem.

9. (Much, Very) few of us enjoyed that meal.

10. I don't go shopping very often (nowadays, recently).

A-2. Correct errors if any:

1. I almost always walk to school.

2. How long ago did you arrive at the station?

3. Always Chieko gets up late in winter.

4. Here our bus comes. Let's get on.

5. At first, mix the eggs and milk, and then, the flour.

6. Almost nothing was done to improve the economic situation.

7. She is playing the piano hardly to win the coming contest.

8. If you don't attend the meeting, I won't too.

9. I don't like her because she talks much.

10. It's still eight o'clock. You aren't leaving already, are you?

B. Fill in each blank with one word to complete the sentence:

1. 一度ファストフード中毒になると止めるのはかなり難しい。

   Once you are addicted to fast food, it is quite (   ) (   ) (   ).

2. 雨が急に激しく降り出したので、彼は親切にも私を自動車で迎えに来てくれた。

   As it (   ) began to rain (   ), he was kind enough to pick me up.

3. 私は昨日仕事に遅れもう少しで首になるところだった。

   I was late for work and (   ) (   ) fired yesterday.

4. 私がこの国に住む決心をした理由の一つはここが暑くも寒くもないからです。

   One of the reasons why I have decided to live in this country is that it's (   ) too (   ) (   ) (   ) here.

5. 1週間前に受けた学期末試験の結果が心配で、昨夜はほとんど眠れませんでした。

   Worrying about the results of the finals I took a week ago, I could (   ) (   ) last night.

6. 最近アメリカに留学する日本の学生が減っている。

   The number of Japanese students who study in the United States (   ) (   ) (   ) decreasing.

7. 私はこの頃洋服はほとんど皆インターネットで買います。

   I buy (   ) (   ) (   ) (   ) on the Internet nowadays.

8. 列車の出発まで後30分しかないのに芳子さんはまだ姿を現していません。

   There is only (   ) (   ) (   ) (   ) the train leaves, but Yoshiko hasn't shown up (   ).

9. 私の知っている中では、小川氏はずば抜けて金持ちな商人です。

Mr. Ogawa is (   ) (   ) (   ) merchant I know.

10. 卒業論文は完全ではありませんが、提出する準備はほとんどできています。

My graduation thesis is not complete, but I'm (   ) (   )
(   ) hand it in.

🎧 *C.* Translate into English:
18

B: 年のせいか以前のように素早く動けない。

A: それもそうだけど、この頃動きがにぶったもう一つの原因は肥満よ。
「肥満」obesity

B: 一生懸命体重を減らそうとしているんだが、僕は肉に目がなくて毎日食べちゃうんだ。
「～に目がない」have a weakness for ~

A: 肉と言えば、最近野菜で作られた「人工肉」が大変評判になっているから試しに食べてみたら。
「人工肉」artificial meat

B: それについては先日新聞で読んだ。その新聞記事によると、これまで「人工肉」を食べたほとんどの人が本物の肉と同じぐらいおいしいっと言っているとのことだ。
「これまで」so far

A: 本物の肉の代わりに「人工肉」を食べて、もっと魚を食べるようにすれば健康にいいわよ。

B: ....
....

A: ....
....

B: ....
....

A: ....
....

B: ....

....

A: ....

....

Unit 10
比較の誤り

▶ 比較級を修飾する副詞は far か much

The overseas market is growing much faster than the domestic market.

🎧 Anime
19

The Japanese anime industry is now worth **more** than $20 billion, and its products are known and loved all over the world. In fact the overseas market is growing **much faster** than the domestic market. However, the industry also faces difficulties, such as copyright infringement and shortage of talent. Many anime artists are overworked and make considerably **less** money than their American 5 counterparts. But this is partly because Japanese anime still rely so heavily on drawing by hand, which in turn is one reason why many people feel they are **better than** American cartoons.

Comparing American cartoons to Japanese anime, many critics have concluded that anime are the **more** interesting. Developing out of the manga tradition, they 10 have **more** diverse themes, plots and styles, and are **more** imaginative. The settings are often **more** realistic, and the human relationships **more** complex. The backdrops to each scene are intricately painted, with incredible attention to detail. Japanese anime are **not so much** entertainment for children **as** serious works of art. Films like Takahata Isao's *Grave of the Fireflies* and Miyazaki Hayao's *The* 15 *Wind Rises* are **more** challenging than entertaining, raising serious issues like war and the constitution.

The great anime director Miyazaki Hayao is considered a national treasure. British filmmaker Terry Gilliam thinks *My Neighbor Totoro* is **the greatest** of all animated films, for its spectacular imagination, while *Spirited Away* overtook 20 *Titanic* to become **the highest-grossing** film in Japanese history. *Spirited Away* has now itself been overtaken by Makoto Shinkai's *Your Name*, and one day his fame may be even **greater** than Miyazaki's.

It could be said that Westerners used to have a **simpler** image of Japan, centered on its feudal "samurai" past, and modern technological achievements like the shinkansen. But with the arrival of anime like Otomo's *Akira* in the late 1980s, followed by the works of Studio Ghibli, people are coming to have a **more** human and complex image of Japanese culture. One could say that anime culture has given Japan a new face. Indeed it was manga and anime characters like Astro Boy, Naruto, Son Goku and Luffy who were chosen as ambassadors for the Tokyo Olympics.

25

30

★ Notes ★

4 **copyright infringement**「著作権の侵害」／ 15 *Grave of the Fireflies*『蛍の墓』／ 15– *The Wind Rises*『風立ちぬ』／ 19 **Terry Gilliam**「テリー・ギリアム」監督作品にアニメ映画『モンティ・バイソン』シリーズなどがある。／ 19 *My Neighbor Totoro*『隣のトトロ』／ 20 *Spirited Away*『千と千尋の神隠し』spirit away「誘拐する、こっそり運び去る」／ 21 *Titanic* 映画『タイタニック』／ 21 **the highest-grossing**「最高の粗収入をあげる」／ 22 **Makoto Shinkai's** *Your Name* 新海誠監督の映画『君の名は』。／ 26 **Otomo's** *Akira* 大友克洋原作・監督の長編アニメ『AKIRA』。／ 29– **Astro Boy, Naruto, Son Goku and Luffy**「鉄腕アトム、ナルト、孫悟空、ルフィ」ナルトもルフィもアニメの主人公の名前。

Watch the words

1. 原則として1音節の形容詞・副詞の比較級は〈原級 +-er〉。

　○ I can run **faster** than Bob.
　× I can run *more fast* than Bob.

　　★ 原則として1音節の形容詞と副詞の比較級は〈原型＋ -er〉。2音節の形容詞と副詞の中にも clever のように比較級は〈原型＋ -er〉のものもある。

2. 3音節以上の形容詞・副詞の比較級は原級の前に more または less をつける。

　○ I think the new President is **more nervous** than he looks.
　× I think the new President is *nervouser* than he looks.

　　★ 2音節の形容詞と副詞の大部分と3音節以上の形容詞と副詞の比較級は、原級の前に more または less を付ける。

3. 比較級を修飾する副詞は far か much。

　○ He is **far smarter** than his brother.
　○ He is **much smarter** than his brother.
　× He is *very smarter* than his brother.

　　★ 比較級を修飾する副詞は far か much で very は用いられない。

4. good の比較級は better。

○ Ken is a **better** tennis player than Pete.
× Ken is a *gooder* tennis player than Pete.
× Ken is a *more good* tennis player than Pete.

> ★ good, bad, much, little の比較級・最上級は不規則変化で、〈原級 +-er〉や〈more+ 原級〉とはならない。better, worse, more, less などはそれ自体で比較級。

5. 同一人物や同一物の性質を比較するときは more と less を用いる。

○ Mary is **more pretty** than beautiful.
× Mary is *prettier* than beautiful.

> ★ 同一人物や同一物の性質を比較するときは、more か less を用いて、〈原級 +-er〉は使わない。

6. fewer は数、less は量の比較に。

○ Goro has **less** homework than Takeshi.
× Goro has *fewer* homework than Takeshi.

> ★ 日本語の「より少ない」は数にも量にも使える表現だが、英語では数の場合は fewer、量の場合は less を用いる。

7. 2 人または 2 つの物の比較は〈the+ 比較級〉で。

○ She is **the taller** of the two.
× She is *taller* of the two.
? She is *the tallest* of the two.

> ★ 2 人または 2 つの物の比較は〈the+ 比較級〉が標準用法。ただし、口語では、最上級が使われることもある。

8. 3 人以上または 3 つ以上の物の比較は最上級で。

○ Caroline is **the youngest** of the three.
× Caroline is *the younger* of the three.

> ★ 3 人以上または 3 つ以上の物の比較では比較級は使えず最上級で表す。

9. 比較の対象は同じものに。

○ My salary is larger than **my brother's**.
× My salary is larger than *my brother*.

> ★ 日本語では「僕の給料は弟より多い」のような比較表現が可能だが、英語では比較の対象は同じものにしないと誤りになる。すなわち、ここで比較しているのは my salary と my brother's salary で、my salary と my brother ではない。

10. 「A よりむしろ B」は not so much A as B。

○ He is **not so much** a teacher **as** a researcher.
× He is *not as much* a teacher *as* a researcher.

★ He is not so tall as Jiro. は He is not as tall as Jiro. のように言い換えられるが（特に、口語では後者の方が一般的だが）、「A よりむしろ B」を意味する not so much A as B は慣用表現なので、not as much A as B とは言えない。

Exercises

A-1. Choose the right words:

1. He is the (most, best) respected politician in this country.

2. The chemistry exam was (less, least) difficult than I had expected.

3. You should study English as (hard, harder) as possible.

4. She is not (as, so) much an announcer as a TV personality.

5. My brother eats twice as (much, more) as I do.

6. This is the (most bad, worst) movie that I have ever seen.

7. Growing up in the country, I don't have the (fewest, least) idea what New York is like.

8. The next (better, best) pitcher on our team is Saburo.

9. He comes to see us when we (less, least) expect it.

10. For (farther, further) information, please call our office in Seattle.

A-2. Correct errors if any:

1. We had fewer rain this year than last year.

2. We went further up the mountain.

3. Everyone thinks John is fastest of the three runners.

4. She is more well-dressed than you.

5. I want to buy a bigger bike than Jim.

6. You have a lot more CDs than I do.

7. I think Janet is more charming than beautiful.

8. The economic situation in Japan is getting more worse than a month ago.

9. Money is least valuable today than it used to be.

10. Mineko is smarter of the two sisters.

B. Fill in each blank with one word to complete the sentence:

1. 私たちのクラスでは健太ほど一生懸命勉強する生徒はいない。

   No other student in our class studies (   ) (   ) Kenta.

2. 私がこれまで見た3つの映画の中ではこれが最高です。

   This is (   ) (   ) (   ) (   ) three movies I have seen so far.

3. その病気は発展途上国で広がっています。

   The disease is spreading in (   ) (   ) countries.

4. 僕のアパートの家賃は君のアパートより安いよ。

   The rent of my apartment is (   ) (   ) (   ) of yours.

5. 私の英語の試験の結果は思っていたより遙かに悪かった。

   The result of my English exam was (   ) (   ) (   ) I had
   expected.

6. 君が本当に欲しいのはペットよりガールフレンドだろう。

   What you really want to have is (   ) (   ) (   ) a pet (   ) a
   girlfriend.

7. ウサギの耳は犬よりずっと長い。

   The ears of a rabbit are (   ) (   ) (   ) (   ) of
   a dog.

8. 彼女は社交的と言うよりおしゃべりなんだ。

   She is (   ) (   ) (   ) sociable.

9. この公園の桜は今が一番きれいです。

   The cherry blossoms in this park are (   ) (   ) at this time of
   the year.

10. 2人の娘の上の方は最近銀行員と結婚しました。

The (　　　　) (　　　) our two daughters has recently (　　　　　) (　　) (　　　　).

20

C. Translate into English:

A: 私はお寺に興味があるので去年来日しました。

B: そうですか。日本ほどお寺の多い国はありませんからね。

A: あなたもよくお寺を訪れるのですか。

B: ええ、少なくとも50のお寺に行ったことがあります。

A: 私はこれまで20のお寺を訪れました。あなたは私より遥かに多くのお寺に行っていますね。

B: 春になったら、法隆寺とか銀閣寺ほど有名ではないけどもっと訪れる価値があると思ういくつかの小さいお寺に連れて行ってあげますよ。

A: ....

....

B: ....

....

A: ....

....

B: ....

....

A: ....

....

B: ....

....

Unit 11
関係詞の誤り

▶ 関係代名詞の所有格は**whose**が最も一般的

***Buddhism is a religion whose teachings
are not deeply understood.***

🎧 Religion
21

It is well known that the Japanese tend not to have exclusive religious beliefs.
When asked **what** their religion is, 70 percent say Shinto, but 70 percent say
Buddhism. Most people also say they do not believe in a deity, or "follow" a religion.
In many countries, people believe in monotheistic religions. These have founders
and teachings **that** tell us how to live. People assemble in churches, mosques, and 5
synagogues, to reaffirm their faith. And religious leaders go around preaching the
"good news" of their religion **to whoever** will listen. In Japan, however, Buddhism
is a religion **whose** teachings are not deeply understood, and Buddhist temples are
primarily seen as places **which** conduct memorial services and funerals.

Are the Japanese just not religious by nature? The modernizers of the Meiji 10
Period looked on religion with some suspicion. Ito Hirobumi thought religion was
nothing more than superstition, and Fukuzawa Yukichi said he himself lacked a
religious nature. When people visit temples and shrines, **which** they do not do
all that often, it is more out of cultural convention than religious belief. It could be
said that **what** little religious belief people have is connected to *kami-no-michi*, or 15
Shinto, **which** is not really a religion, but a form of animism. It celebrates human
life, sees purity in nature, and finds gods in natural objects—for example in trees,
rocks, and mountains. The natural sites **where** people felt a mysterious presence
were consecrated as shrines.

This attitude to life used to be widespread in the ancient world. Indeed, Greek 20
philosophers like Thales said all matter is alive and full of gods. In Japan, people
saw souls in inanimate objects. *Kuyo* ceremonies were conducted to lay to rest the
souls of objects like dolls, and even the tools **with which** people worked, like

knives and needles. It was as though these objects had consciousness. Today, some physicists say consciousness may actually permeate the universe and interact with matter at the quantum level. The animism of Shinto, then, could be said to be in tune with the modern world. It may provide clues as to how we can coexist with nature, and also bridge the gap between science and religion.

★ Notes ★

3 **deity**「神」／ 4 **monotheistic religion**「一神教の宗教」／ 16 **animism**「あらゆる事物や現象には無形の霊魂があるとする信仰」／ 19 **were consecrated**「崇められた」／ 21 **Thales**「タレス」古代ギリシャの哲学者で自然哲学の創始者。／ 25 **permeate**「浸透する」／ 26 **quantum**「量子」

Watch the words

1. 先行詞が「人＋物」または「物＋人」のときの関係代名詞は that。

○ Did you see the car and the driver **that** collided with the bus?
× Did you see the car and the driver *who* collided with the bus?
× Did you see the car and the driver *which* collided with the bus?

★ 先行詞が「人＋物」または「物＋人」のとき、関係代名詞に who や which は使えず、that を用いる。関係代名詞の that は、先行詞に「唯一」や「全て」の意味の修飾語が付いている場合も好んで使われる。

2. 先行詞を含む関係代名詞は what。

○ Tell me **what** you want to buy.
× Tell me *which* you want to buy.
× Tell me *that* you want to buy.

★ 先行詞を含む関係代名詞は、関係代名詞に ever がついた複合関係代名詞を除けば what だけ。関係代名詞の which や that は先行詞を必要とする。

3. 日本語に引かれて前置詞を抜かさないように。

○ The toys **with which** you are playing are made in Germany.
× The toys *which* you are playing are made in Germany.

★ この文の play は自動詞なので、「おもちゃで遊ぶ」は play with a toy。従って「あなたが遊んでいるおもちゃ」は the toy with which you are playing と関係代名詞の前に前置詞の with を入れないと誤りになる。

4. 関係代名詞の所有格は whose が最も一般的。

○ He goes to a university **whose tuition** is high.
○ He goes to a university **the tuition of which** is high.

× He goes to a university *which tuition* is high.
× He goes to a university *that tuition* is high.

> ★ 関係代名詞の所有格は先行詞が人で物でも whose が最も一般的。先行詞が物の場合は of which も正用法ではあるが、whose の方が好んで使われる。

5. 文全体を先行詞とする which。

○ I'm going to a concert, **which** I seldom do.
× I'm going to a concert, *that* I seldom do.

> ★ 前の文全体または一部を先行詞とする非制限用法の関係代名詞は which だけで、that は使えない。

6. 場所の後に使われる関係詞はいつも where とは限らない。

○ This is the new park **which** attracts lots of young people.
○ This is the new park **that** attracts lots of young people.
× This is the new park *where* attracts lots of young people.

> ★ 場所の後に使われる関係詞はいつも where と覚えている学生が多いが、関係詞の導く節の中で、その語が副詞の働きをしていれば関係副詞の where を、代名詞の働きをしていれば関係代名詞の which か that を使わなければ誤りになる。

7. 関係副詞はいつ使う？

○ I visited the house **where** the late prime minister was born.
○ I visited the house **in which** the late prime minister was born.
× I visited the house *which* the late prime minister was born.

> ★ 先行詞が場所のとき、関係詞の導く節の中で、その語が副詞の働きをしている場合は関係副詞の where か〈in+ 関係代名詞の which〉を使う。

8. the way how という表現はない。

○ That's **how** I solved the problem.
× That's *the way how* I solved the problem.

> ★ the reason why とは言えるが、the way how という表現はない。関係副詞を用いない That's the way I solved the problem. は正しい英語である。

9. what は関係形容詞としても使われる。

○ I gave the poor boy **what** little money I had.
× I gave the poor boy *that* little money I had.
× I gave the poor boy *which* little money I had.

> ★ what は「…するすべての」の意味の関係形容詞として使われる場合ある。特に、few, little を伴って「少ないながらあるだけの」の意味で用いられることが多い。

10. 関係代名詞の格はその働きにより決まる。

○ I would like to give these books to **whoever** wants them.
× I would like to give these books to *whomever* wants them.

★ 関係代名詞の格は、関係代名詞が導く節の中での働きにより決まるので、前置詞の後でも目的格がくるとは限らない。

Exercises

A-1. Choose the right words:

1. I have a dog (which, whose) name is Pochi.

2. (That, What) the professor said today is very important.

3. This is the knife (which, with which) he killed his neighbor.

4. Last night I took my sister to the movies, (that, which) I seldom do.

5. Everything (that, which) you consider to be important should be bought today.

6. I don't believe (that, what) you say.

7. He is (that, what) is called a genius.

8. I was born in the year (which, when) World War II ended.

9. She told the rumor to (whoever, whomever) called her.

10. I gave him everything (that, which) I had in my pocket.

A-2. Correct errors if any:

1. Tell me that you want to eat for dinner.

2. I have learned what little I know by trial and error.

3. The subject which I am interested is chemistry.

4. The condo where he is living in now is close to the campus.

5. That's what rugby differs a lot from football.

6. The boy and his dog who were crossing the road were hit hard by a car.

7. Yesterday we visited the park where is famous for its tulips.

8. She is no longer what she used to be.

9. Solar energy is an idea that time has come.

10. All what glitters is not gold.

B. Fill in each blank with one word to complete the sentence:

1. 君が今しなければならないことは一生懸命勉強することだ。

   (   ) (   ) (   ) (   ) do now is to study hard.

2. あなたが必要な手助けは何でもしますよ。

   I'll give you (   ) (   ) you need.

3. 私たちは欲しい人には誰でもマスクをあげますよ。

   We will give masks (   ) (   ) wants them.

4. 彼女は君を利用するようなタイプの人ではありません。

   She is not the type of person (   ) (   ) advantage of you.

5. テッドを知っている誰が、彼が医科大学に入ったと信じるか。

   (   ) (   ) (   ) Ted would believe that he has entered a medical college?

6. 彼は僕の友人の1人が最高経営責任者の会社に勤めています。(「最高経営責任者」chief executive officer = CEO)

   He works for a company (   ) CEO is one of my friends.

7. 私がこの写真を撮ったカメラは日本製です。

   The camera (   ) (   ) I took this photograph is made in Japan.

8. これは彼が重要な役割を果たした試合でした。

   This was the game (   ) (   ) he played an important role.

9. 彼が地球温暖化の権威であり、多くの人が尊敬しているカナダ人の科学者です。

   He is a Canadian scientist (   ) (   ) an authority on global warming and (   ) many people respect.

10. ディーゼルエンジンは汚染物質を排出し、そのことが人々の健康に悪い影響を与えています。

    Diesel engines produce pollutants, (   ) (   ) a bad influence on people's health.

C. Translate into English:

B: 先月 2 年振りに新潟の故郷へ帰ってきた。

A: そう。あなたの生まれた家はまだそのままだった？

B: いや、去年父がリフォームして雰囲気が全く変わっていた。

A: よく一緒に釣りに行った旧友の誰かに会った？

B: 今地元の銀行に勤めている秀樹に会った。僕は酒はあまり好きじゃないので、滅多にしない
ことなんだが、酒場へ行って 1 時間以上も話をした。

　　「酒場」bar

A: 彼は父が大手商社の重役の女性とまだ付き合っているの？

　　「〜と付き合う」go out with 〜

B: ....

....

A: ....

....

B: ....

....

A: ....

....

B: ....

....

A: ....

....

Unit 12
接続詞の誤り

▶「と」は **and** とは限らない

Many visitors to Japan would be hard put to decide which they prefer, its culture or its nature.

🎧 Nature
23

Many visitors to Japan would be hard put to decide which they prefer, its culture **or** its nature. They visit cultural sites in Kyoto **and** enjoy the tranquil atmosphere of its temples and shrines. But they also go hiking in Japan's national parks **and** are delighted by the magnificent scenery they encounter there. Japan is remarkable in being almost 70 percent covered by forests. It has a high level of biodiversity, 5 with nearly 1,000 species of trees, **and** great natural beauty, with large areas of sparsely-inhabited mountains, fast flowing rivers, gorges, **and** spectacular stretches of coastline.

The Japanese themselves often see a "love of nature" as part of their identity. Japanese literature is full of natural images, **for** the Japanese closely identify their 10 feelings with natural phenomena. Nature speaks to people's hearts. *Waka* and *haiku* contain many references to the seasons, to cherry blossoms, as well as to rain, dew, insects and flowers, **because** they evoke *mono-no-aware*, the ephemeral nature of things. The Japanese may have less affinity with wild nature, **but** feel a deep connection to nature on a human scale. In the past, rural communities lived in close 15 harmony with nature. In the *satoyama*, local forests were carefully nurtured, water resources husbanded, and biodiversity protected. **Whether** people lived **or** died depended on how well they could exploit nature without destroying it. **As** they could not travel great distances, they had to become experts at knowing the potential and the limitations of their local environment. 20

In the Meiji Period, the Japanese embraced Western technology **because** they did not see it as a threat or foresee the consequences. Later, there was severe pollution of the air, seas, rivers, and soil, **while** riverbanks and mountainsides were covered with concrete. **One reason** for this may be **that** nature was no longer thought to have any economic value. Today, **howeve**r, the global environment is under extreme stress. We have to find new ways of living in harmony with nature, **or** it will be too late. **As** a recent initiative by the Japanese government has proposed, the Japanese *satoyama* could serve as a model for a locally-based, sustainable economy in which nature is protected.

★ Notes ★

1 **hard put to** ～「～するのが難しいと分かる」／ 7 **sparsely-inhabited**「人がまばらに住んでいる」
／ 13 **ephemeral**「はかない、束の間の」

Watch the words

1. 「と」は and とは限らない。

○ Which do you like better, summer **or** winter?
× Which do you like better, summer *and* winter?

★「A と B とでどちらが好きか」と問う場合の「A と B」は、A or B で、A and B は誤り。

2. 2 つの逆接関係の節を結ぶ等位接続詞は but。

○ Kenji passed the history exam, **but** I failed it.
× Kenji passed the history exam, *and* I failed it.

★ 2 つの逆接関係の節を結ぶ等位接続詞は but で and は使えない。

3. 命令文の後の and と or の使い方。

○ Get up right away, **or** you'll be late for school.
× Get up right away, *and* you'll be late for school.

★ 命令文あるいは命令文に準ずる表現の後の「そうしなければ、さもないと」に相当する英語の接続詞は or で、and は「そうすれば」の意で用いられる。

4. 「A も B ない」は not A or B か、neither A nor B。

○ I do **not** smoke **or** drink.
○ I **neither** smoke **nor** drink.
× I do *not* smoke *and* drink.
× I *neither* smoke *or* drink.

★「A も B ない」は not A or B か、neither A nor B で、not A and B や neitherA or B は誤り。not A and B が使われるのは、You should not drink and drive. のように A と B が密接な関係にあるか行為が同時に行われる場合だけ。

5. for は理由を述べる格式張った表現。

○ We have to leave now, **for** we have a long way to go.
○ We have to leave now, **because** we have a long way to go.
× We have to leave now, *so* we have a long way to go.

> ★ for は理由を述べる格式ばった等位接続詞で、口語では because を使うのが一般的。so は、前の文章を受け、「それで、それゆえ」の意で用いられる等位接続詞。

6. 理由を表す as と so は普通一緒には使えない。

○ **As** I was poor, I couldn't buy a car.
× *As* I was poor, *so* I couldn't buy a car.

> ★ 一般的に、as が理由を述べる接続詞として使われるとき、主節に更に so を付けるのは誤り。接続詞の as と so が同時に使われるのは、As rust eats iron, so care eats the heart. (錆が鉄を食するように苦労は人の心を食する) のように様相を表すときだけ。

7. 「が」はいつも but とは限らない。

○ I went to see the ball game yesterday **and** enjoyed it very much.
× I went to see the ball game yesterday *but* enjoyed it very much.

> ★ 日本語では、「…したが…だった」という表現をよく使うが、この「が」は英語では but ではなくて and。

8. The reason is because .... は書く英語では避けた方がよい。

○ One of **the reasons** for our success was **that** we conducted market research carefully.
? One of *the reasons* for our success was *because* we conducted market research carefully.

> ★ 名詞主語の reason に応ずる補語は名詞節が普通で、The reason is that .... が正用法。The reason is because .... という表現は口語ではしばしば用いられるが書く英語では避けた方がよい。

9. if 節は主語や補語にはなれない。

○ **Whether** we should go on strike is the biggest decision we have to make.
× *If* we should go on strike is the biggest decision we have to make.

> ★ whether と if は、She asked me if [whether] I attended the meeting. のような文で は交換可能だが、if で始まる節は主語や補語にはなれない。また、if 節は前置詞の目的語にはなれない。

10. 正しい because の使い方。

○ I refused to join the club **because** its regulations were too strict.
× I refused to join the club. *Because* its regulations were too strict.

> ★ 文章で because で始まる節が後ろにくるとき、前の主節をピリオドで終え、後の節を Because で始めて文を独立させるのは誤りである。Because 以下は従属節だからである。

ただし Why did you miss the English class yesterday? という質問に対し、Because I was sick in bed. と答えるような場合はI missed the English class yesterday. が略されているのが明らかなので誤りではない。

Exercises

A-1. Choose the right words:

1. It must have rained last night (but, for) the ground is wet this morning.

2. I have three brothers (and, but) they are all doctors.

3. It's not hot (and, or) muggy today.

4. He is neither tall (nor, or) good-looking, yet I like him.

5. (If, Whether) he was hurt in the accident is not known yet.

6. Which country do you like better, Sweden (and, or) Spain?

7. The train was 15 minutes behind schedule, (as, so) I was late for school this morning.

8. The success depends on (if, whether) he is in good shape.

9. (As, When) we reached Osaka, we got in touch with Professor Wright.

10. (As, Because) everyone knows, the government's plan to raise taxes is unpopular.

A-2. Correct errors if any:

1. As I got home, I called my mother living in the country.

2. He never eats pork nor beef.

3. Which do you like better, meat or fish?

4. I am reading the book you lent me the other day, but it's very interesting.

5. The question is if the government should raise taxes again.

6. As he grew older, he became more selfish.

7. I came home earlier than usual. Because it was getting cold.

8. The phone rung just as I was leaving the office.

9. Don't drive so fast, and you'll cause an accident.

10. Two more days, and the summer vacation is over.

B. Fill in each blank with one word to complete the sentence:

1. この前の日曜日にピクニックに行ったんだが、とても楽しかった。

   I went on a picnic last Sunday, (   ) (   ) enjoyed it very much.

2. あなたは「郷に入りては郷に従え」という諺を知らないのですか。

   Don't you know the proverb (   ) says "When in Rome, do (   ) the Romans do."?

3. 一生懸命勉強しなさい、さもないとあなたが選んだ大学の入学試験には合格しませんよ。

   Study hard, (   ) you (   ) (   ) pass the entrance examination to the college of your choice.

4. 今日の午後は雨になりそうなので家にいます。

   (   ) it looks like rain this afternoon, (   ) stay home.

5. 私は昨日その野球試合をに見にいかなかったし、彼女も行かなかった。

   I didn't go to see the baseball game yesterday, and she (   ) (   ).

6. 明日運動会が開かれるかどうかは天気次第です。

   (   ) the athletic meet (   ) (   ) tomorrow depends on the weather.

7. ガソリンが車に必要なように、水は我々に必要だ。

   (   ) gasoline is necessary for cars, (   ) water is for us.

8. 図書館は夜 11 時まで開いているので家へ帰る前にそこで数時間勉強できます。

   The library stays open (   ) eleven at night, (   ) I can study there for a few hours before I go home.

9. 彼が大学を中退したのは勉強が嫌いだったからではなく授業料がもう払えなかったからです。

   He left college (   ) (   ) he didn't like studying (   ) (   ) he couldn't pay his tuition any more.

10. 明日の試合に相手チームのエースが登板するかどうかは問題ではありません。大事なことは私たち全員が一致団結して彼に立ち向かうことです。

It doesn't matter (　　　　　) or (　　　　) the ace pitcher of the opposing team will pitch in tomorrow's game. (　　　　) (　　) important is (　　　) all of us hang together and stand up to him.

C. Translate into English:

A: あなたは大学を卒業してからここ数年1人で住んでいるが寂しくないの。

B: うん、でも寂しいときはステレオでクラシック音楽を楽しんでいる。

A: 犬か猫を飼うことを考えたことはないの？　かわいいよ。

B: いや、ないね。犬も猫もあまり好きじゃないんだ。

A: 気の毒な人ね。犬でも猫でも飼ってごらんなさい、あなたのよい友達になって君が1日の忙しい仕事から帰ってきた時に元気づけてくれるわよ。

B: 地方へ転勤になって少し仕事が楽になったら、犬を飼うのを考えてみるよ。犬の方が猫より人間に忠実だそうだから。

A: ....

....

B: ....

....

A: ....

....

B: ....

....

A: ....

....

B: ....

....

Unit 13
前置詞の誤り

▶ 「朝に」は常に in the morning か？

The era of the samurai came to an end on the morning of September 24, 1877.

🎧 *Bushido*
25

Bushido is sometimes called an "invented tradition," since the term was not much used **until** the Meiji period, and the samurai had almost disappeared **by** that time. Yet samurai did have an unwritten code of conduct. They had to be ready to die for the sake of honor, and to commit suicide **by** *seppuku* if they were defeated or disgraced. According to the "*Hagakure*," we may die this morning, and should 5 constantly be mindful of mortality. Even during the Edo period, a samurai could kill someone **with** his sword if he felt his honor had been compromised. This was, of course, a very grave matter. If a samurai took someone's life, he had to stay at home **for** 20 days to reflect on what he had done.

The era of the samurai came to an end **on** the morning of September 24, 1877, 10 when Saigo Takamori was killed after leading a rebellion against the government. But Saigo was still praised **for** his traditional samurai virtues. In the Meiji period, foreign culture and customs were pouring **into** Japan, and scholars like Nitobe Inazo reminded people **of** the positive virtues of *bushido*, which could help Japan compete with the West. Later, as Japan moved **in** the direction of militarism, bushido 15 was used to encourage soldiers to sacrifice themselves for the Emperor, and children were taught that *bushido* made Japanese culture superior **to** Western culture.

One might think that *bushido* has nothing to do with our peaceful modern era, and **in** another few decades it will have been forgotten. Yet the fighting spirit of *bushido* still survives in the martial arts, in baseball, and even soccer. After all, the 20 national football team is called "Samurai Blue." Meanwhile, "corporate warriors" show great self-sacrifice and loyalty to their companies. Besides, *bushido* was deeply concerned with matters other than warfare. Samurai were expected to show

strength of character **by** practising virtues like justice, learning, self-control, and
compassion towards the weak. Today, we find "character-building" emphasized in ₂₅
the mottoes of universities, many of which were founded by ex-samurai. We should
not forget that *bushido* owed much to Neo-Confucianism, and sought to create an
orderly, peaceful society, in which violent conflict was minimized.

★ Notes ★

5 *"Hagakure"*『葉隠』元佐賀藩士による武士の道徳を説いた書。1716 年完成。／ 20 **martial arts**
「格闘技」／ 21 **corporate warriors**「企業戦士」／ 26 **ex-samurai**「元サムライ」

Watch the words

1. 「までに」は by、「まで」は till か until。

- ○ I'll finish my homework **by** tomorrow morning.
- × I'll finish my homework *till* [*until*] tomorrow morning.

   ★ by は「までに」という期限を示し、till と until は「まで」という動作・状態の継続を示す。

2. 時間の継続を表す for。

- ○ I have lived in Tokyo **for** 18 years.
- × I have lived in Tokyo *in* 18 years.
- × I have lived in Tokyo *since* 18 years.

   ★ 前置詞の for は、期間を示す言葉の前に付けて、ある動作や状態がその全期間を占める場合
   に使われる。in は、I was born in 2000. のように年月、季節の前で「ある時期」につい
   てか、We can do it in an hour. のように「ある時間以内で」の意味で用いられる前置詞。
   since は「…以来」の意で since this morning などのようにある時点を示す語句とともに
   用いる。

3. 必要な前置詞の欠落。

- ○ She **asked me for advice**.
- × She *asked me advice*.

   ★「人に何かを聞く [尋ねる]」は May I ask you a question? のよう、ask someone something の形を取るが、「人に何かを求める」という意味で ask を使う場合は ask someone
   for something と something の前に前置詞の for を入れないと誤りになる。

4. 内部への動作を示す前置詞は into。

- ○ I have recently gained weight and cannot get **into** these pants.
- × I have recently gained weight and cannot get *in* these pants.

   ★ 内部への動作を示す前置詞は into で、in はある場所や物の中にある静止の状態を示す。

5. 「朝に」は常に in the morning か？

○ We left Tokyo for San Francisco **on** the morning of March 26, 2010.
× We left Tokyo for San Francisco *in* the morning of March 26, 2010.

★ 日にち、曜日に限定されない「朝」、「午後」、「夕方」はそれぞれ、in the morning, in the afternoon, in the evening だが、限定されると前置詞は on が正用法。

6. 副詞句に前置詞を付けてはならない。

○ I got up early **this morning**.
× I got up early *in this morning*.

★ this morning, this week, last week, next Sunday などが副詞句として使われるとき、その前に前置詞を付けてはならない。

7. 道具・材料は with で。

○ He cut meat **with** a sharp knife.
× He cut meat *by* a sharp knife.

★ 道具や材料を使ってという意味の「…で」は with で、by は動作を行った者の前に付く。

8. 「一週間経ったら」は in a week。

○ I'll be all right **in** a week.
? I'll be all right **after** a week.

★ 「（これから）1 週間経ったら」のように未来の時間を言うときの前置詞は in が一般的だが、実際には after も使われている。

9. 「…の方向へ」を to the direction of ... とするのは誤り。

○ They were walking **in** the direction of the library.
× They were walking *to* the direction of the library.

★ 日本語の「…の方向へ」に引かれて to the direction of ... としがちだが、このときの前置詞は in で、to は誤り。

10. superior than ... とは言えない。

○ Jim thinks he is superior **to** us because he is rich.
× Jim thinks he is superior *than* us because he is rich.

★ inferior, junior, senior, superior などラテン語からきた形容詞の比較の後の前置詞は than でなくて to。

Exercises

A-1. Choose the right words:

1. It's difficult to get laundry to dry (in, on) a rainy day.

2. (During, In) my stay in the United States, I visited five national parks.

3. This tour is so popular that it will be full (by, till) the end of this month.

4. Once you get (in, into) this forest, you are in a lost world.

5. This song is familiar (to, with) everyone in this country.

6. He cut the tree (by, with) an axe.

7. I am sick and tired (of, with) his selfish attitude.

8. Bread is made (from, of) flour, baking powder and salt.

9. Can you finish your homework (for, in) an hour?

10. He lives (on, with) 1,000 yen a day.

A-2. Correct errors if any:

1. Car accidents have been decreasing in these days.

2. When I started working here, I was junior than everyone else.

3. The certification test is offered several times in a year.

4. Dick passed away in the morning of June 1.

5. Smoking is bad to your health.

6. I've been working for this company for ten years.

7. My grandfather is hard of hearing.

8. When I got in the taxi, I dropped my cell phone.

9. I'm going to take a few days off in the end of this month.

10. We solved the difficult problem with his help.

B. Fill in each blank with one word to complete the sentence:

1. 上野公園は桜で有名で、いつもこの時期は花見客で一杯です。

   Ueno Park is famous (　　　　) its cherry blossoms and crowded (　　　　)
   blossom viewers (　　　　) this time of the year.

2. 昇進したら東京の郊外に庭付きの家を買いたい。

   I'd like to buy a house (　　　　) a garden (　　　) a suburb of Tokyo when I get
   promoted.

3. 切符を買っている間子供たちを見ていてね。

   Please (　　　　) your eye (　　　　) the children while I am buying tickets.

4. 先日３人の登山者が落石で死にました。

   Three climbers were (　　　　) (　　　　) falling rocks the other day.

5. 今まで数学がどれほど難しいか気づきませんでした。

   (　　　　) now I (　　　　) not realized how difficult mathematics is.

6. 宮里教授は今朝東京を発ちロンドンへ向った。

   Professor Miyazato left Tokyo (　　　　) London (　　　　) morning.

7. 私が病院に見舞いに行ったとき彼はベッドに横になっていました。

   He was lying (　　　　) the bed when I visited him (　　　　) the hospital.

8. 私がテレビで映画を見ていたとき母は突然私の部屋に入ってきた。

   Mother suddenly came (　　　　) my room when I was watching a movie
   (　　　) TV.

9. 彼は、酔っ払い運転は自ら災難を招くようなものだという私たちの警告を無視してハイウエーであの大事故を起こした。

   Ignoring our warning that drunken driving is just asking (　　　　) trouble, he
   caused a big accident (　　　) the highway.

10. 私は30分ほど前にジャックとスージーが腕を組んで公園の方向へ歩いて行くのを見たよ。

    I saw Jack and Susie walking arm (　　　) (　　　　) (　　　　) the direction of
    the park about half an hour (　　　　).

26

C. Translate into English:

A: 考えてみてよ。後2週間で夏休みよ。

B: 一学期はあっという間に終わるね。

「あっという間に」in a flash

A: 今夏の計画は何かあるの？

B: 初めて海外旅行をしようと思っているんだ。君は外国へ行ったことがあるかい？

A: 高校時代にカナダへ行った。英語は得意だと思っていたけど、英語で自分を理解してもらうのに苦労したわ。

B: 僕は、大学へ入ってからずっと勉強で忙しかったから、気分転換に箱根の温泉に行ってゆっくりしたい。

「気分転換に」for a change

A: ....

....

B: ....

....

A: ....

....

B: ....

....

A: ....

....

B: ....

....

Unit 14
主語の選択、語順、態、否定などの誤り

▶ 「遅かれ早かれ」はlater or soonerとは言わない

But sooner or later sumo was bound to recover.

 Sumo

Training for sumo, Japan's national sport, is extremely intensive. Junior wrestlers must practice hard from 5 AM, as well as eating massive meals twice a day so that **they can gain weight**. They live in dormitories, are not allowed to have girlfriends or drive cars, and face serious health problems later in life. Nevertheless, sumo has attracted trainees from all over the world since Hawaiians like Takamiyama arrived in the 1960s. **He and others**, like Konishiki and Akebono, achieved huge success. By 1992, when **six young Mongolian wrestlers** entered the Oshima stable, sumo had become so popular with foreigners that the Sumo Association had to limit their numbers.

Sumo went on to suffer a number of scandals. **It had never occurred** to most fans that matches might be "fixed," as happens in professional wrestling, or that wrestlers might be involved in illegal gambling. And **little did anyone know** that bullying took place in sumo stables, until a trainee was beaten to death in 2007. Later, a wrestler **was seriously injured** after being assaulted by a *yokozuna*. But **sooner or later** sumo was bound to recover. Recently, the wrestler Kisenosato became the first Japanese to be promoted to *yokozuna* for many years, and sumo has now regained its popularity with the public, to the point where it is difficult to obtain tickets.

For foreigners, if they are **lucky enough** to arrive in Japan during one of the 3 annual tournaments, a visit to the Kokugikan at Ryogoku can be a magnificent day's entertainment. One can watch bouts all morning, then order a *bento* and **something cold** to drink **before the real excitement starts** around 4 PM. Huge wrestlers face off in their elaborate *mawashi* and topknots, throw salt into

5 10 15 20

the ring, and stamp their feet to purify the ground. Then there is an explosion of activity, and one of the *rikishi* crashes to the floor. Afterwards they bow to each other, showing no emotion whether they win or lose. It is as though time has stood still, and one is back in the Edo era. In this globalized age, **not many countries can boast** a national sport that is such a unique and colorful spectacle.

★Notes★

5– **Takamiyama, Konishiki, Akebono**「高見山」「小錦」「曙」それぞれハワイ出身の力士名。「高見山」と「小錦」は大関に、「曙」は横綱に昇進した。／ 7– **Oshima stable**「大島部屋」／ 11 **fixed**「不正に仕組まれた」八百長のこと。／ 15 **Kisenosato**「稀勢の里」／ 21 **bouts**「(相撲の)取り組み」／ 23 **topknots**「まげ」／ 24 **ring**「土俵」／ 25 **crashed to the floor**「地面(土俵)にどすんと倒れる」

Watch the words

1. 日本語と英語で主語が違うことがある。

○ **I have** recently **gained weight**.
× *My weight* has recently *gained*.

★ 日本語では、「最近体重が増えちゃった」のように言うが、英語では My weight has recently gained. とは言えない。この場合の gain の主語は I でないといけない。

2. 自動詞は単独では受動態を作れない。

○ When **did** the idea **occur** to you?
× When *was* the idea *occurred* to you?

★ 自動詞は、前置詞や副詞と結びついて他動詞的に用いられるときは、He was laughed at by his classmates. のような受動態は可能だが、単独では受動態は作れない。

3. 日本語の能動態が英語では受動態のことがある。

○ He **was injured** while he was playing football.
× *He injured* while he was playing football.

★ 「怪我をする」、「喜ぶ」、「驚く」、「満足する」などは日本語では能動態だが、英語ではそれぞれ be injured、be pleased、be surprised、be satisfied のように受動態で表す。

4. 日本語は否定文でも英語は肯定文のことがある。

○ Let's go home before it **starts** raining.
× Let's go home before it *doesn't start* raining.

★ Let's go home before it starts raining.（雨が降り出さないうちに家に帰ろう）、I answered only three of the 10 questions.（私は10問中3問しか答えられなかった）などの文では日本語が否定になっていても英語は肯定文である。

5. 「僕と先生は」は I and the teacher ではない。

○ **The teacher and I** discussed global warming.
× *I and the teacher* discussed global warming.

★ 日本語では「私と先生は」と言えるが、英語では何か悪いことをしたとき以外は必ず the teacher and I と I が後にくる。日本語では「父と息子」、「息子と父」、「母と娘」、「娘と母」などどちらの語順でも使われるが、英語ではそれぞれ father and son, mother and daughter の語順で用いるのが普通である。

6. -thing, -body, -one で終わる語の修飾語は後置される。

○ I would like to drink **something cold**.
× I would like to drink *cold something*.

★ something cold, somebody rich, someone special のように、-thing, -body, -one で終わる語を修飾する場合形容詞は後に置かれる。

7. 形容詞の並べ方には順序がある。

○ **Five young American** students called on me yesterday.
× *Young five American* students called on me yesterday.

★ 形容詞がいくつか並ぶとき、その順序は原則として (1) 冠詞・代名形容詞、(2) 数量、(3) 大小、長短、(4) 性質、(5) 老若、新旧、(6) 所属、材料。

8. 副詞の enough は形容詞・副詞の後にくる。

○ He was **kind enough** to show me the way to the station.
× He was *enough kind* to show me the way to the station.

★ 形容詞の enough は被修飾語の前にも後にもくるが、副詞の enough は常に形容詞や副詞の後で使われる。

9. 英語独特の語順。

○ **Sooner or later**, she will learn the lesson.
× *Later or sooner*, she will learn the lesson.

★「衣食住」は food, clothing and housing、「貧富」は rich and poor、「老若」は young and old、「遅かれ早かれ」は sooner or later で、英語と日本語とでは逆の語順だが、これらは慣用表現なのでこの語順を変更することはできない。

10. 強意のための倒置。

○ **Little did I know** that he was an illegal entrant.
× *Little I knew* that he was an illegal entrant.

★ 上例のように否定の副詞（句）またはそのほか強調する語句を文頭に置いた場合は倒置が起こり、be 動詞（それ以外の動詞の時は助動詞）が次にきて、それから主語が続く。

Exercises

A-1. Choose the right words:

1. He is not (enough old, old enough) to drink.

2. We serve (bread and butter, butter and bread) in the morning.

3. I asked him (how far he can throw, how far can he throw) the ball.

4. Prices are determined by the forces of (demand and supply, supply and demand).

5. Rarely (I open, do I open) the door to that room.

6. Two criminals (escaped, were escaped) from the prison early this morning.

7. (Will you take it, Will it take you) a long time to finish writing your report?

8. There is (nothing wrong, wrong nothing) about your plan.

9. Let's finish cleaning this room before my sister (comes, doesn't come) home.

10. The (father and son, son and father) next door are always quarreling.

A-2. Correct errors if any:

1. Gone are the days when we lived in peace.

2. I'm very thirsty and want to drink cold something.

3. Do you know where was the accident happened?

4. Do you satisfy with your present salary?

5. I have seen more fireworks this evening than I can remember.

6. There was anybody in my class who didn't come up with a better plan than this one.

7. My father pleased with his new car.

8. Please let me know when do you come to Japan.

9. She will learn a lesson from this mistake, later or sooner.

10. After the oil crisis followed a long period of economic stagnation.

B. Fill in each blank with one word to complete the sentence:

1. 東京へ着いたのは夜遅かったが、親切にも大学時代からの親友の健司が空港に迎えに来てくれた。

   I arrived at Tokyo late at night, but Kenji, a close friend from college, was ( ) ( ) ( ) meet me at the airport.

2. 雄一が昨夜列車事故で怪我をして入院したと聞いて驚いた。

   I ( ) ( ) ( ) hear that Yuichi ( ) ( ) ( ) a train accident and hospitalized last night.

3. 私の友人の1人は読み切れないほどマンガ本を持っている。

   One of my friends has ( ) comic books than he ( ) ( ).

4. 気の毒にその家族は当時衣食住を確保するのに大変苦労していました。

   At that time, the poor family was having a lot of difficulty in securing ( ), ( ) and ( ).

5. この前の土曜日私と父は日本の将来について1時間近く話し合った。

   ( ) ( ) ( ) ( ) discussed the future of Japan for nearly one hour last Saturday.

6. 人類の歴史上今ほど地球温暖化が大問題になっていることはありません。

   At no time in the history of mankind ( ) global ( ) posed such a serious problem as it does today.

7. 遅かれ早かれ老いも若きもこの歌の虜になるでしょう。

   ( ) or ( ), people ( ) and ( ) will be captivated by this music.

8. 彼にはどこも悪いことはないのだから、なぜ彼が来春地方の小さな支社にとばされるのか誰にも分からない。

   Nothing is wrong with him, so nobody can understand why he is to be transferred to a ( ) ( ) ( ) ( ) ( ).

9. 週末に彼女と軽井沢へ小旅行するんだ。今度の土曜日が待ち遠しいよ。

   I'm going to take ( ) ( ) ( ) ( ) ( ) ( ) ( ) over the weekend. I can hardly wait for next Saturday.

10. 先日評判の占い師に運勢を見てもらったわ。彼は、私は遠からず誰か有名な人と知り合いになると言っていた。

I had my fortune told by a popular fortune teller the other day. She said I would get acquainted (　　　) (　　　　) (　　　　) in the not-too-distant future.

C. Translate into English:

A: 先日たまたま、外国から来た若くて背が高くてハンサムな2人の観光客に会ったわ。

B: そう。どこから来たのか尋ねた？

A: ええ。1人はフィンランドからで、もう1人はスウェーデンから来たの。彼らが日本や日本の物事についてよく知っているのを知って驚いた。それにひきかえ、私は彼らの国のことはほとんど知らなかったので恥ずかしかったわ。

　　「それにひきかえ」in contrast

B: 僕だって両国に関する知識はあまりないよ。唯一知っていることはそれらの国の貧富の差が他の多くの先進国に比べて小さいことだ。

A: それは両国の国民がとても高い税金を払っているためなの？

B: そうだが、彼らは教育や病気や老後の生活の費用を心配する必要がないから自分たちの政府の政策には満足しているようだよ。

　　「老後の生活」life in their old age

A: ....

....

B: ....

....

A: ....

....

B: ....

....

A: ....

....

B: ....

....

Unit 15
身体に関する表現の誤り

▶「腹」は **stomach** だが。

It only gets their backs up.

🎧 *Minka*
29

Although we must **keep in mind** that Japanese homes cannot be built of brick or stone, because Japan suffers from earthquakes, modern houses are generally not built to last long. Once they are more than 30 years old, they have scarcely any value. The traditional *minka*, however, is an under-appreciated treasure of Japanese culture. Built out of wood by highly skilled craftsmen, using elaborate joining techniques and hardly any nails, some *minka* are still standing after 150 years. 5

If you live in a remote area of the countryside, you can see beautifully-crafted *minka* everywhere. It is like having a museum of rural life **right under your nose**. Yet there are said to be several hundred thousand of them standing empty. Many are in a poor state of repair, and have to be demolished. They are so well- 10 constructed that it **breaks your heart** to see them being torn down. Still, it is better to **bite your tongue** than try to persuade people not to destroy old minka. It only **gets their backs up**, since they have already **racked their brains** to find a solution to the problem. After the original residents have died, old houses are troublesome and expensive to maintain, and younger family members are often not 15 in a position to live in them.

Many foreigners in Japan dream of living in a rural *minka*. For those **with long arms and legs**, it can be difficult to duck under low beams, or sit on tatami mats without suffering pain in the **lower back**. But this is more than compensated for by the beauty and natural materials of the building. Once you have a lot of contacts 20 in a rural area, it is relatively easy to acquire a *minka* to live in. If you ask a carpenter to convert the interior and modernize it, he may **shake his head** and say the job is too difficult and time-consuming. However, if you are prepared to do the work yourself, these fine old buildings can be converted into comfortable modern homes. As more people become able to "telework" from home, perhaps restoring *minka* in this way may also help to solve the crisis of rural depopulation. ₂₅

★**Notes**★

18 **duck under low beams**「低い梁に頭をひょいと下げる」

Watch the words

1.「頭」は head とは限らない。

　○ Keep **in mind** that you have to report to the university once a month.
　× Keep *in the head* that you have to report to the university once a month.

　　★「頭に入れておく」、「頭をひねる」、「頭にくる」などは英語では head を使わず、それぞれ keep in mind、rack one's brain、get on one's nerves や get mad at someone など と言う。

2.「首」「胸」などに head が使われることがある。

　○ He **shook his head when I asked him if he had seen my wallet on the table**.
　× He *shook his neck when I asked him if he had seen my wallet on the table*.

　　★ 日本人は、否定をする動作を「首を振る」と言うが、英語ではこのとき neck でなく head を使い、shake one's head と言う。「（威厳や自信を示して）胸を張る」は英語では hold up one's head。

3.「顔」は face を使って訳せないときがよくある。

　○ He **knows a lot of people**.
　× His *face is wide*.

　　★「苦虫をかみつぶしたような顔をする」などの「顔」は英語でも face を用いて make a sour face と言えるが、「顔が広い」に face は使えない。「（会合などに）顔を出す」も make an appearance で face は用いない。

4.「目」が nose ？

　○ I didn't notice my watch on the table, although it was **right under my nose**.
　? I didn't notice my watch on the table, although it was *right before* my eyes.

　　★「すぐ目の前」という表現は英語では right under one's nose の方が right before your eyes より一般的。「目先のことしか考えない」も cannot see beyond (the end of) one's nose。「目がいい」は have good eyes ではなく have good eyesight。

5. 「口」はよく tongue と訳される。

○ **Hold your tongue**, or you'll get fired.
× *Hold your mouth*, or you'll get fired.

★ 「口が悪い」、「口をつぐむ」「口を慎む」などの場合は mouth でなくて tongue を使い、それぞれ have a sharp tongue、hold [bite] one's tongue、watch one's tongue と言う。

6. 日本語の「手」は hand も arm も含む。

○ Generally speaking, Americans have longer **arms and legs** than the Japanese.
× Generally speaking, Americans have longer *hands* and legs than the Japanese.

★ 人体を表す言葉に関しては、日本語は大まかで、「手」は英語の hand（手）と arm（腕）の両方を指すことがあるが、英語にするときは arm か hand か見極める必要がある。

7. 野球用語の「肩が強い」は have a strong arm。

○ Our catcher has a strong **arm**.
× Our catcher has a strong *shoulder*.

★ 「肩」は普通 shoulders で、raise one's shoulders（肩を上げる）、shoulder to shoulder（肩を寄せ合って）のように使うが、「肩が強い」のときの「肩」は英語では arm だ。「人に肩を貸す」は give [lend] someone a hand で、この場合も shoulder は使えない。

8. 「胸」は heart で表すことがよくある。

○ My **heart** almost broke with sadness.
× My *chest* almost broke with sadness.

★ 「胸」は「（胸を打って）悲しむ、得意がる」、「胸を打たれる」などの表現では beat one's breast, be shot in the chest のように breast や chest が使えるが、「胸が裂ける」「胸が高鳴る」、「胸の内を明かす」などというときの「胸」は heart。

9. 「腹」は stomach だが。

○ His arrogance got my **back** up.
× His arrogance got my *stomach* up.

★ 「腹が痛い」や「腹ばいになる」の「腹」は stomach をそのまま用いることができるが、「腹を立たせる」は get somenon's back up、「腹を割って話す」は have a heart-to-heart talk で stomach は使えない。

10. 難しい「腰」の英訳。

○ I have a pain in my **lower back**.
× I have a pain in my *waist*.

★ 和英辞典を引く「腰」のところで waist が目に付くが、waist は「人の腰に手を回す」、「腰回り」などと言うとき以外はあまり使われない。「腰が痛い」は have a pain in one's lower back、「腰を曲げる」は bend one's back だ。

Exercises

A-1. Choose the right words:

1. Tell me what you have in (head, mind).

2. He is a gentleman at (heart, stomach).

3. I can't make (brain, head) or tail of why my grandson has drawn.

4. Don't poke your (neck, nose) into my business.

5. He is the type of guy who has a (finger, hand) in many pies.

6. Sandra is tall and has long, slim (feet, legs).

7. I was so shocked by the news that I had trouble finding my (mouth, tongue).

8. His arrogant attitude always gets on my (head, nerves).

9. My brother has a good (brain, head) and learns everything very quickly.

10. Why do you always take Mike's (shoulder, side)?

A-2. Correct errors if any:

文尾の（ ）内の日本語を参考にすること

1. Don't put your neck out of the train window. （首を出す）

2. Sorry, I stepped on your leg. （足を踏む）

3. My shoulder is stiff. （肩がこる）

4. The territorial issue has been giving Japan a headache. （頭痛の種）

5. He is head over heels in love with her. （首ったけ）

6. I know him only by face. （顔を知っている）

7. My sister has eyes for works of art. （見る目がある）

8. When I threw the ball, the dog tried to catch it with his feet. （両足で）

9. The fire was out of hands when the fire engines arrived. （手がつけられない）

10. She turned a deaf ear to our request. （耳を貸さない）

B. Fill in each blank with one word to complete the sentence:

1. あの野球選手の運動能力には頭が下がります。

   I take my (　　　　) (　　　　　　) to the baseball player for his athletic ability.

2. 岡田氏は未だ若いのに新しい首相の右腕です。

   Mr. Okada is still young, but he is the (　　　　　　　) (　　　　　) of the new prime minister.

3. 彼が私の兄の悪口を言ったので頭にきました。

   I (　　　　) (　　　　　) (　　　　　) him for saying bad things about my brother.

4. 順番を待っているとき胸がどきどきしていました。

   My (　　　　　) was pounding while I was (　　　　　) (　　　　) my turn.

5. 私が彼にその話をしたとき、彼は首を傾けた

   When I told him the story, he tilted (　　　) (　　　　　).

6. ここは舗装してない道だから足下に注意して。

   This is a dirt road, so (　　　　　) (　　　　) (　　　　　).

7. 腹を割って話し合えばたいていの問題は解決できるよ。

   We can solve almost all our problems if we have a (　　　　　　　　　)
   (　　　　).

8. 学校当局はいじめの問題を解決すべく知恵を絞っています。

   School authorities are racking (　　　　　) (　　　　　) trying to solve the problem of bullying.

9. あなたは目がいいからあんな遠くの看板の文字も読めるんですよ。

   You have (　　　　) (　　　　　　), so you can read the letters on such a distant sign.

10. 広島の原爆ドームを見たときわたしは胸に熱いものがこみあげてきました。

    I felt a lump (　　　) (　　　) (　　　　　　) when I saw the Atomic Bomb Dome in Hiroshima.

30

C. Translate into English:

A: ちょっとお腹が出てきたようね。

　　「腹が出る」 get a little potbelly

B: うん、以前より在宅勤務が増えて、運動不足で体重が増えちゃったんだ。

A: 朝か晩、あなたの家の近くにある大きな公園を散歩したら？ 歩くのは体にいいわよ。

B: それは分かっているんだけど、僕は腰に問題を抱えていてね。

A: 私の友人の1人も長い間腰痛で悩んでいるんだけど、この前会ったとき、毎日の、ちょっとした散歩のおかげで幾分状態がよくなったと言っていた。

B: 君の忠告を頭に入れて、時間のあるときは歩くようにするよ。

A: ....

....

B: ....

....

A: ....

....

B: ....

....

A: ....

....

B: ....

....

Common Errors in English Writing
New Edition

読み・書く 英語表現のポイント15章

編著者	木 塚 晴 夫
	Roger Northridge
発行者	山 口 隆 史

発 行 所　　　株式会社 音羽書房鶴見書店

〒113-0033　東京都文京区本郷 3-26-13
TEL 03-3814-0491
FAX 03-3814-9250
URL: https://www.otowatsurumi.com
e-mail: info@otowatsurumi.com

2021年 3 月 1 日　　初版発行
2023年 3 月15日　　4 刷発行

組版　ほんのしろ
装丁　オセロ 大谷治之
印刷・製本　（株）シナノ
■ 落丁・乱丁本はお取り替えいたします。

ISBN978-4-7553-0052-3　　　　　　EC-075